S0-AGO-651

Given to

_____

on the _____ *day of* _____

from

_____

MORE BEAUTIFUL
BEAUTIFUL
than
DIAMONDS

OTHER BOOKS BY THE AUTHOR

The Gift of Family: A Legacy of Love

MORE BEAUTIFUL

than

DIAMONDS

The Gift of Friendship

NAOMI RHODE

THOMAS NELSON PUBLISHERS
NASHVILLE

4th Reprint: Oct. 1997

Published in Nashville, Tennessee, by Thomas Nelson,
Inc.

Printed in the United States of America.

Scripture quotations are from the NEW KING JAMES
VERSION of the Bible. Copyright © 1979, 1980, 1982,
Thomas Nelson Publishers, Inc.

Library of Congress Cataloging-in-Publication

More beautiful than diamonds : the gift of
friendship / Naomi Rhode.
p.   cm.
1. Friendship.   I. Title.
BJ1533.F8R48   1990
177'.6—dc20
90-28468
ISBN 0-8407-7459-1   CIP

Printed in the United States of America
4 5 6 7 8 9 BVG 01 00 99 98 97

Acknowledgments

· ·

I wish to acknowledge my parents, who instilled the ideals of friendship within me;

Nido Quebin and Og Mandino, who encouraged me to share the story within me;

Ed Pepin, who believed in and facilitated the project for me;

My husband, Jim, and friends, who are the reality of the richness of friendship to me; and

Georglyn Rosenfeld, who has researched and compiled materials for me.

Contents

· ·

In life . . .
the most essential thing
for happiness
is the gift of friendship.

SIR WILLIAM OSLER

A Legacy of Gifts

 My love of friends came from the first true friends I ever had, my mother and father. The loss of my parents at an early age (my father when I was 13 and my mother when I was 23) magnified their influence on my life and formed a "friend-shaped vacuum" that I joyfully spend my life filling. The friends who have helped fill that vacuum have truly become like precious gifts to me.

One of my goals in life is to offer the gift of my friendship to as many people as possible and stimulate others to interact in these relationships. As a result, I have received many wondrous gifts of friendship.

After my parents died, I was heartbroken and lonely. I hung on to every remembrance of them as well as the attitudes and values they instilled in me. Although they were not rich in material wealth, they left me with a mental, emotional, and spiritual legacy that money could not buy.

The letters they sent me as a young woman, the kind of role models they were, and the life experiences they shared with me are intricately woven into the fabric of my life. Above all they gave me the gift of their friendship. Some of the last words my mother spoke to me were, "You have been the most wonderful daughter a woman could ever have and one of my very best friends." She also gave me some wonderful advice about friendship and family life that I will share throughout this book and in the book *The Gift of Family: A Legacy of Love.*

My mother's engagement ring was given to me. It is a beautiful diamond I cherish next only to my own engagement diamond. I was given my father's journals, notebooks, and sermon notes and a book of "Memory Gems" he collected—an incredible legacy of his thoughts, philosophy, and the essence of his person. Throughout this book I will liberally scatter many of the quotes from my father's collection.

Although I am quoting hundreds of sources, I am not necessarily endorsing or recommending everything written by that person or in that book. However, I do like the particular thoughts I choose to share with you and I want to thank each of the exceptional people whose very special quotes fill these pages.

Every attempt has been made to give credit and secure permission for the use of these quotes. When the same quote was attributed to several people, I tried to find the correct source. Some sources were unknown as my father just wrote down thoughts he loved, not where he found them. If I have made a mistake or omitted credit, please inform the publisher in writing and the correction will be made in future editions of the book.

In this book I want to share with you some stories and facts about the many similarities I find between friendships, gifts, and diamonds. My wish is for you to be unable to look at a diamond again without thinking of some special friend or loved one, what he or she means to you, and what kind of a gift you can give to that person.

I think diamonds are one of the most beautiful gifts nature has provided us. Yet there is something far more beautiful than diamonds; the beauty and special joy our friends can bring to us and that we give to them. I would like to share with you some of the beautiful relationships I have been privileged to experience—relationships that have stood up under the most rigorous of tests and proved genuine—in the hope that I might help you improve and increase the quality and reality of the friendships and relationships in your life. Friends truly are more precious and more beautiful than diamonds.

I love to give gifts and love to encourage everyone else to give gifts. This book is my gift to you. Not only is it a gift in and of itself, but the messages it offers are a gift within a gift. My philosophy is "everything you paid for and a little bit more" and I hope that's what you feel you've gotten after reading this book.

. . . .

PART ONE

A
Gift Wrapped in Diamonds

. . . .

Giving as a Life-style

✦ A Gift Wrapped in Crackerjacks ✦

Rings and jewels are not gifts, but apologies for gifts.
The only true gift is a portion of thy self.
EMERSON

*M*y very first diamond came out of a Crackerjack box. I was eight years old and the special gift took my breath away. My enthusiasm and imagination caused it to sparkle for me, reflecting the myriad of colors in my mind. Although it was only an inexpensive glass chip, I wanted to believe it was real and for me, it was!

I thought maybe someone in the Crackerjack factory in Chicago got tired of putting cheap little gadgets in each box and said, "This is a very special present. . . . I know some very deserving little girl will appreciate it."

Magically I had selected the special box at that store and knew it had been put there especially for me as a wonderful reward just for being "me."

I wore the ring for a few days before realizing it was turning my finger green. It wasn't real after all, but that didn't dampen my enthusiasm. I was happy to receive it, to wear it, and to look at it. I loved it and it was mine.

Consequently, I consumed an inordinate amount of Crackerjacks as a child. I wasn't especially fond of them, but I kept hoping to find another diamond ring in the box. I never did, but each box contained a special prize—a gift. Even if I didn't have any use for the gift, I felt special because someone had given *me* something. Receiving an unexpected gift, no matter how mundane, was exciting for me and apparently for millions of other children who consumed Crackerjacks.

Recently, I heard about a young man whose girlfriend also loved Crackerjacks and invariably looked for her gift by dumping out all the Crackerjacks as soon as she opened the box. He carefully opened the bottom of a box of Crackerjacks, inserted a real diamond ring, and sealed the box back up. During a family party everyone received a box of Crackerjacks. She rummaged through looking for her prize and found a real diamond engagement ring!

Gifts are one of my favorite things. I love to give them and I love to receive them. However, I have learned that the best gifts are when we give of ourselves.

✦ *The Art of Giving* ✦

*W*e give of ourselves when we give gifts of the heart—love, kindness, joy, understanding, sympathy, tolerance, forgiveness.

We give of ourselves when we give gifts of the mind—ideas, dreams, purposes, ideals, principles, plans, inventions, projects, poetry.

We give of ourselves when we give gifts of the spirit—prayer, vision, beauty, inspiration, peace, faith.

We give of ourselves when we give the gift of the word—encouragement, inspiration, guidance.   PETERSON

✦ *Lagniappe* ✦
. . . .

We make a living by what we get; we make
a life by what we give.
DUANE HULSE

*M*y philosophy of giving started with a story my father
told me when I was just eight years old . . . the story of a shopkeeper who during the Depression days chose to be different
from other people. In doing so he would very carefully weigh
out your commodity, your coffee beans, for example, in his
scale, so that the five pound weight and the container of coffee
beans were absolutely equal. Then he would pause and smile,
twinkling at his customer, put the scoop back in the bag of
beans one more time and fill the container to overflowing so
that it would off balance in favor of the customer. Then he
would say "lagniappe," which in French Creole means,
"everything that you paid for and just a little bit extra." In so
doing he was guaranteeing that his business would be success-
ful amidst the Great Depression because he gave even when he
himself was in need.

The shopkeeper practiced the old philosophy of "Give, and
it will be given to you. A good measure, pressed down, shaken
together and running over, will be poured into your lap. For
with the measure you use, it will be measured to you." Although it is a basic principle for all of us to live by, it is hard to
find the lagniappe philosophy in practice in today's world but it
is how we need to approach our friendships.

✦ *Being a Bargain Friend* ✦

*L*ord, help me to be a "bargain" friend. By that I mean, let those who come to me for friendship get more than they expected.

For what they give me in friendship, Lord, let me remember to try to give them still more.

Let them always go away from me surprised at the fullness of their hearts.

Let them always be pleased at the measure they have received from me. And remind me never to put my thumb on the scale when I am weighing out my love to them.

Let me always put an extra something, an unexpected pleasure, into the hours they spend with me.

Let me give them my best service and freest credit.

Let me keep my doors open to them at all hours.

Let my thoughts and words, which are my commodities, be always fresh and appealing.

May my friends never come to me for understanding and find it out of stock.

Let them never come to me for companionship and find it to be of poor quality.

May they never find my friendship to be more than they can afford, or even as much as they can afford.

Remind me never to deceive them with false advertisements of myself.

Thus, help me to be a "bargain" friend, O Lord, always.

And then if I find at last that I have given to them more than I've gotten in repayment, then I shouldn't at all mind going out of business that way.   JAMES ALEXANDER THOM

✦ How Should We Give? ✦

So let each one give . . . not grudgingly or of necessity; for
God loves a cheerful giver.

2 CORINTHIANS 9:7

*M*any years ago I had a friend I'll call Joyce. It seemed like
I was Joyce's only friend, so when she became sick and had to
be hospitalized I felt I should be there as much as possible.
Little did I know how much of a commitment my friendship
with Joyce would involve! Over a period of twelve years, Joyce
was in and out of the hospital continually. I tried to be there for
her though the return benefit seemed zero because she was totally preoccupied with her disease.

One day Joyce said she wanted me to have her Wurlitzer
organ when she died. I love to play the organ and was thrilled
at the thought of receiving it. Perhaps I even felt a twinge of
satisfaction—as if I were finally going to receive some "payment" for all my time, love, and attention.

Several months later Joyce expressed her realization of her
nearness to death and her need to get rid of her possessions. She
placed an ad in the paper to sell her fur coat and her organ. I
was speechless and disappointed.

After considerable suffering and an extended hospital stay,
Joyce died. No one said anything to me about her Wurlitzer
organ and I assumed it had been sold.

Joyce's funeral was a sad day. I would miss my "one-sided
friendship." I went to the small church where the funeral was
held, a church with a small budget and large financial problems. There on the platform was "my" organ. The organist
played beautifully, bringing comfort to the hearts of everyone
in the congregation as she filled the auditorium with music,
all from "my" organ. After the service I noticed a small gold
plaque commemorating Joyce's gift to the church dated shortly
after Joyce had spoken to me about disposing of her possessions.

I was forced to stop and analyze my true motives. Initially I
visited Joyce in the hospital because I felt she had no one else.
Did I continue visiting her to guarantee my "gift" of the organ,
or did I really care for Joyce in her lonely vigil?

While I was assuring myself that I really cared for Joyce regardless of the organ, I remembered Luke 12:48: "For everyone to whom much is given, from him much will be required; and to whom much has been committed, of him they will ask the more." To stay in balance, my giving must keep pace with my riches. I had so much; Joyce had so little. I loved Joyce's Wurlitzer organ but I didn't need it; the church did. It now thrills me to realize that every Sunday beautiful music is played on "my" organ and enjoyed by a congregation who could not otherwise have afforded an organ.

I had received a "gift" from Joyce, the "gift" of learning that the magic of giving comes when we abandon the idea of reciprocation or currying favor. In giving with abandon, we are most richly rewarded.

✦ *Friendship Involves Giving and Receiving* ✦

Friendship involves the sharing of the selves.
And one of the greatest aspects, certainly,
of love is joy in personal life.
Each friend must be able to give that joy
and to enter into it. . . .
The very idea of a worthy friendship
implies that the friends need
and desire each other
and so are continuously receptive
and eager for the other's gift.

HENRY CHURCHILL KING

✦ Is It Easier to Give Than to Receive? ✦

. . . .

It is more blessed to give than to receive.

ACTS 20:35

*A*ccepting a gift can require talent. While it's better to give than to receive, it may also be easier. In fact, the way we accept a gift is a gift in and of itself. Accept a gift graciously—even if we don't particularly like it.

I have a friend who went to Tahiti. Before the trip, the travel agent told her to bring along a few gifts to give to those who served her well. In Tahiti offering money as a tip was an insult, but giving gifts was greatly appreciated. While in Tahiti, my friend especially enjoyed smiling at and laughing with Octave, a waiter in her hotel, who served her meals everyday. Although he spoke only French and she spoke only English, they managed to communicate through smiles and laughter. When she was ready to leave, she gave Octave a T-shirt worth about twenty dollars as a thank-you for his thoughtfulness and service and asked to have her picture taken with him.

In return, he attempted to give her a very expensive tiki statue—a statue she had seen in the gift shop, very much wanted but hadn't bought because it cost sixty dollars. When she got the message across to him that she couldn't accept it because it was so expensive, he turned with a disappointed look on his face and did not even say good-bye. The interpreter explained that by not accepting the gift he offered, she had insulted him.

My friend protested that the tiki statue cost three times more than the T-shirt and she thought it was too much money for a "poor" waiter to spend on her. After all, she was trying to reward him for his good service and certainly didn't expect a gift in return. The interpeter told her he was not a "poor" waiter. His father was Tahiti's Minister of the Interior, and it was a great compliment that he had offered such a nice gift to her as a token of friendship.

One month after she returned home, a box of twenty shell necklaces was delivered to her at her office. They were from the waiter. This gift was repeated each year for three years. The postage for sending each box was over twenty dollars. Can you imagine? *He* was sending *her* presents because she'd hurt his feelings!

*I*t is more blessed to give than to receive. . . . [But] the givers who cannot take in return miss one of the finest graces in life, the grace of receiving. . . . To receive gratefully from others is to enhance their sense of their worth. It puts them on a give and take level, the only level on which real fellowship can be sustained. . . . It changes one of the ugliest things in the world, patronage, into one of the richest things in the world, friendship.

HALFORD E. LUCCOCK

✦ A Gift Wrapped in Diamonds ✦

Do not neglect the gift that is in you. . . .
1 TIMOTHY 4:14

A few years ago after I had an incredibly rough speaking engagement, my husband, Jim, gave me a necklace that was a replica of a little gold gift box with a bow of diamonds.

The real gift, however, was what he told me: "I want you to always remember when you wear it and touch it that there is a gift inside. The gift is the reminder that you are loved regardless of who disagrees with you. Remember, you don't have to please everybody. You are not responsible for how everyone perceives you. You don't know where they are coming from or what they've just experienced. There will always be someone in each audience that you are there for specifically. Reach those you can reach and don't let the others upset you."

It sounded very close to a philosophy my father had carved in wood and placed at the entrance to the Boy Scout Camp where he was summer director: "They say what they say, let them say."

For years I wore the little gold gift box with a diamond bow every time I spoke and always thought of the special gift inside. It was a gift wrapped in diamonds. Much of life is the same. We find many gifts within a gift.

I never cease to be amazed at the beauty of nature and its marvelous gifts to us. A special treat from nature is the wonderful diamonds it has hidden in the earth. I love the sparkle they add to my life. They are a fun part of my enjoyment of life and all its beauty.

Yet my diamonds are not the outward trappings of a poseur or a pseudosophisticate. Like the gift box, they are a visible symbol of the way I approach life. They are precious because of what they mean to me, not the effect they have on others. They are precious because, like my marriage, family, and friends, they are thoroughly genuine. They are an ever-present material reminder of the infinitely greater, nonmaterial value of the lasting relationships I've established in my life; a gift box wrapped around a treasure of far greater worth.

✦ The Power of Giving ✦
. . . .

With the death of every friend I love . . . a part of me
has been buried . . . but their contribution to my
happiness, strength, and understanding lives
on to sustain me in an altered world.
HELEN KELLER

*W*hen fifteen-year-old Felipe Garza, Jr., learned that his
fourteen-year-old girlfriend, Donna Ashlock, needed a heart
transplant he told his mother he was going to die and that he
wanted Donna to have his heart.

Three weeks later, on January 7, 1986, a blood vessel burst
in Felipe's brain and his heart was transplanted into Donna.

As relatives sobbed and linked arms around Felipe's open
coffin, the Reverend Thomas Cargo of the Sacred Heart Catho-
lic Church referred to Felipe's gift of his heart to his ailing
girlfriend as proof that all of us have the power to give life to
others.

"Today, we have a concrete example of a heart being left
behind," said the Reverend Cargo. "Let this death, let any
death that touches us be just as much a hope to let life continue.

"We celebrate a moment that is both joyful and sad; we celebrate a moment that is life-giving and life-threatening. Felipe's
passing shows all of us have the power to give, now and even in
our own deaths."

✦ The Gift of Friendship ✦
. . . .

*T*o have a friend is to have one of the sweetest gifts; to be a
friend is to experience a solemn and tender education of soul
from day to day. A friend remembers us when we have forgotten ourselves. A friend may praise us and we are not embarrassed. He takes loving heed of our work, our health, our aims,
our plans. He may rebuke us and we are not angry. If he is
silent, we understand. It takes a great soul to be a friend. . . .

One must forgive much, forget much, forbear much. It costs time, affection, strength, patience, love. Sometimes a man must lay down his life for his friends. There is no true friendship without self-sacrifice. We will be slow to make friends, but having once made them, neither life nor death, misunderstanding, distance, nor doubt must ever come between.

UNKNOWN

✦ *The Priceless Gift* ✦

*F*riendship is a priceless gift
That cannot be bought or sold
But its value is far greater
Than a mountain made of gold
For gold is cold and lifeless
It can neither see nor hear
And in the time of trouble
It is powerless to cheer
It has no ears to listen
No heart to understand
It cannot bring you comfort
Or reach out a helping hand.
So when you ask God for a gift
Be thankful if He sends
Not diamonds, pearls or riches
But the love of real true friends.

HELEN STEINER RICE

. . . .

PART TWO

Maximizing Your Investment

. . . .

The Value of Diamonds and Friends

✦ Friends Affirm Our Worth ✦

> What a priceless gem is a friend! A jewel whose lustre the
> strong acids of poverty and misfortune cannot dim.
>
> UNKNOWN

*N*ot long ago in Miami Beach, Florida, a seventy-year-old woman was walking across the lobby of a bank when her foot kicked something. She picked up the filthy, grimy object, cleaned it off, and discovered it was a diamond ring with two small diamonds and an enormous square one just over a half inch in size. She wasn't sure if the diamonds were real, so she took it to a jeweler, who appraised the 11.78 carat diamond ring to be worth $225,000.

After talking to an attorney, she turned the ring over to the Miami Beach Police Department. She was told that the ring would be hers if no one claimed it within ninety days. The police sent news of the ring out on a nationwide law-enforcement network and also checked for wealthy clients with safe-deposit boxes at Sun Bank.

On the eighty-ninth day a strong lead arose, which the police checked out for ten days before rejecting the claim. Miami Beach Police affirmed that the $225,000 diamond belonged to the woman who found it, even if the original owner turned up.

Although the woman thought the ring was valuable, she needed someone to appraise the ring and affirm its value for her. Everyone we know (including ourselves) needs praise and affirmation occasionally. By affirming others, we affirm ourselves. When we give away joy and encouragement, those reinforcers come back to us, through the act of making another person feel great about him or herself! When we cast our bread upon the waters it comes back buttered! Give the gift of affirmation every day. Give and you will receive.

✦ *A Tribute to Friendship* ✦
. . . .

*F*riendship. There's something so special about that word.

The world bows to people who have so committed themselves to each other.

In honor of friendship wars have been fought and won, fortunes have been given away, crowns have been relinquished.

In service to friendship we stand vigil at the bedside of the dying, adopt orphans, care for widows and clothe the needy. Friendship brings warmth to a shivering beggar, company to the lonely and laughter to the hurting.

In commitment to friendship men and women have been burned at the stake, torn apart by lions, maimed, imprisoned, and martyred.

In tribute to friendship symphonies have been composed, classics written and masterpieces painted.

It is a word of respect and awe, a word of prayer and hope. It is love in its rarest, most selfless form . . . friendship.

MARY HOLLINGSWORTH

✦ *Friends Stick Around* ✦

There is no possession more valuable
than a good and faithful friend.

SOCRATES

*S*ome friends of mine owned a retail store in a beautiful resort town in New Mexico. Financially they did well until the Texas and New Mexico economy took a nose-dive along with the prices of oil and real estate, and the failure of several large banks and savings and loan institutions added to the financial chaos. Like dominoes collapsing, the businesses in this small town seemed to fall one after another because they were so dependent upon each other paying their bills.

It wasn't just a business relationship however, most of the residents were also friends. Many of those who experienced failure were unable to face their friends because they could not pay their debts. Many of them quietly filed bankruptcy and moved out of town at night without telling anybody good-bye.

One family in the town, realizing that relationships are more valuable than resources, threw a bankruptcy party. They sent out party invitations to all their friends. The invitations read:

> UNFORTUNATELY, we are going to file bankruptcy this week. FORTUNATELY, our friends are our most valuable assets and we realize it now more than ever before. Please drop by this Friday night and affirm your friendship at a time when we so desperately need it. P.S. Please bring your own food and drink.

✦ Spendthrifts ✦
. . . .

 *N*ever cast aside your friends if by any possibility you can retain them. We are the weakest of spendthrifts if we let one friend drop off through inattention or let one push away another or if we hold aloof from one for petty jealousy or heedless slight or roughness. Would you throw away a diamond because it pricked you? One good friend is not to be weighed against the jewels of all the earth. If there is coolness or unkindness between us, let us come face to face and have it out. Quick, before the love grows cold. Life is too short to quarrel or carry black thoughts of friends. It is easy to lose a friend, but a new one will not make up for the loss of the old one. ANONYMOUS

✦ A Heart Outside Your Own ✦
. . . .

Friendship hath the skill and observation of the best
physician, the diligence and vigilance of the
best nurse, and the tenderness and
patience of the best mother.
EDWARD CLARENDON

 *S*ocial support, meaning positive interaction among people, has proven to have a powerful impact on an individual's mental and physical well-being.

In a large study of about 7,000 California adults aged thirty to fifty-nine, a strong correlation between social "connectedness" and length of life was found. Having friends also seemed to account for protection against ailments such as heart disease, cancer, and circulatory problems.

People with few social ties had between two and five times the mortality rate of those who were better connected. Pregnant women under stress without supportive, close personal relationships had three times the number of complications. Twenty-eight percent of widows—but only 4.5 percent of married women—complained of chest pains, shortness of breath, infections, and headaches. Rates of mental hospitalizations were five to ten times greater for separated, divorced, or widowed persons than for married individuals who we assume have a good friendship with their spouse. Being connected to others was found to have a more positive impact on one's health than the negative effects of smoking, drinking, lack of exercise, or poor diet. The last sentence is worth rereading!

By caring about others, we are more likely to engage in such positive health behaviors as exercise, medical checkups, and health screening tests. Married people, for example, suffer less illness than single people. There are fewer accidents among married people than among people living alone. This is why insurance companies increase their rates for the separated or divorced.

To my way of thinking, if an insurance company is going to agree to give me lower rates when I get married, there must be some provable benefit in sharing one's life with another.

The bottom line is that those of us who are involved with the lives of others are simply more *alive*. We're involved in life; we're experiencing and doing and growing and changing and learning. It makes sense.

Every friend adds a new dimension to your own emotional health because every friend is a unique gem whose properties contribute their own particular joy.

✦ *Your Friendship Is the Treasure in My Life* ✦

*T*here are treasures in one's life
   that cannot be seen,
cannot be touched,
   are impossible to measure
or estimate their value. . . .
They cannot be bought,
   yet are given for free.
These precious gifts
   have been given to me
and have made a difference in my life
   through the friend I've found in you.

Understanding—of all our different ways.
Honesty—about what you think and feel.
Laughter—at the times we've shared.
Patience—with my changing moods.
Your friendship is among the treasures of my life—
growing as we grow, changing for the better,
yet remaining a steady part of my days.

KATHI ZACK

A man must get friends as he would get food and drink for
nourishment and sustenance. He must keep them as he
would health and wealth, as the infallible safeguards
against misery and poverty of spirit.
RANDOLPH BOURNE

*T*he diamond market has increased steadily for a half century
in the face of all kinds of financial volatility in other markets. It
is not unusual to find investment-quality stones increasing in
value an average of 21 percent in a given decade, with flawless
stones escalating even faster. But how does one measure the
increase in value of a friendship? We just grow richer and
richer.

With both friends and diamonds, there are strict limitations
on what is considered good quality and worthy of the investment of our time and attention. Some diamonds are more valuable than others. Some friends are more valuable to us than
others.

A diamond is measured by the "four Cs": cut, color, clarity,
and carat-weight. Only five different cuts are recommended for
investors: round or brilliant, marquise, pear, emerald, and
oval. In any cut, there should be fifty-eight facets cut to precise
calculations. The color of a diamond generally ranges from absolutely colorless to yellow, and clarity is the flawlessness of a
stone. And obviously, the more carats a diamond has, the
heavier it is, the more valuable it is.

Often, it's tempting and even natural to use similar standards to measure human beings. They must be in our social
strata and they can only be a certain personality type, skin
color, or age. They must be virtually flawless. The problem is,
such narrow limits don't work so well when trying to figure out
who would make a good friend. A good photographer's model,
maybe, but not necessarily a good friend.

Admittedly, and for good reason, the limits are narrow on
investment-quality diamonds. But who determines the parame-
ters on investment-quality friends? Unfortunately when we
judge people by surface qualities such as appearance, wealth,
power, and status we overlook their inner qualities of wisdom,

courage, compassion, integrity, and humor. Mentally, we tell ourselves we would never make a friend or a potential friend conform to some arbitrary, confining standard, but every day we rule out potential friends because we think they don't have enough value to merit our investment.

I am privileged to have circles of friendships, networks of support. A very special group of friends is my "chabre" group—which in Hebrew means "drawn together by cords of love." Six of us meet two or three times each month to support, care, share, and pray for each other. We share our deepest joys and cry together over hurt and pain. They enrich me, help center me, love me, and hold me responsible for growth. I am thankful for this group.

The investment of yourself in another is one of the most basic of all needs. It broadens the confines of our souls to deposit a little of our spirit in others who, in turn, give us the gift of depositing a little of themselves in us. There is no gift more valuable than that.

✦ *Life Is Sweet* ✦

*L*ife is sweet just because of the friends we have
made and the things which in common we share;
We want to live on not because of ourselves, but because
of the people who care;
It's giving and doing for somebody else—on all that
life's splendor depends.
And the joy of this world, when you've summed it all
up, is found in the making of friends.

EDWARD A. GUEST

✦ Friends Are Like Deposits in the Bank ✦

The better part of one's life consists of his friendships.
ABRAHAM LINCOLN

*M*y brother often reminded me that "friendship is like a bank account: you cannot continue to draw on it without making deposits." Some bank accounts are kept active by automatic deposits of one's paycheck. Other bank accounts are set aside for special purposes: a child's college education, a dream vacation, or retirement. Friends are like money in the bank. We make deposits of ourselves and our time into their lives and when we need to make a withdrawal, the friend is there.

My friend Carol and I haven't lived close to each other for over twenty-five years, but we maintain our friendship by seeing each other maybe once a year, sending an occasional letter, or sending a cassette tape to each other. We don't see each other as often as we'd like, but when we're together, it's like we were never apart.

Some friends are needed on a daily or weekly basis. Others are only needed once a month, once a year, or even once every couple of years. But we must continue to make those deposits, whether it is a holiday greeting, a birthday card, notification of major events or changes in one's life, or just a "thinking of you" card in order to keep the friendship open and active.

Even banks close accounts they consider dormant.

. . . .

PART THREE

A Diamond
in the
Rough

. . . .

Finding Friends

✦ Finding Friends ✦

To find a friend one must close one eye—to keep him, two.
NORMAN DOUGLAS

*T*he expression "a diamond in the rough" brings to mind a variety of pictures: something found in an imperfect state, needing a little repair or tender loving care to bring out its true beauty. Do you realize that, in ancient times, all diamonds were left in the rough? It was the diamond's property as the hardest substance on earth that first attracted attention, not its beauty.

I urge you not to overlook precious stones because they are diamonds in the rough. We've all done that.

Twenty years ago I met and had brief social contact with a man I quickly decided was not my type of friend. I found everything about him objectionable and had no desire to associate with him. Recently I was with one of my new friends and we were talking about mutual acquaintances. This man's name came up and my new friend told me he was one of her best friends. I was totally shocked. She too had disliked him initially but was thrown into a working situation with him where she had to get over this animosity.

She made a special attempt to get to know him—went to lunch with him several times and invited him and his wife over to their home for dinner. In about six months a wonderful relationship started to form and twenty years later she considers both him and his wife among her closest and most valued friends. After she was able to overlook the lack of smooth edges of this diamond in the rough, she found a real gem. When she has found herself in need, he has more than proven his faithfulness as a friend both to her and her children.

Were my eyes ever opened! I had overlooked what might have been a meaningful friendship in my life too.

✦ Mining for Diamonds ✦

We are all travellers in the wilderness of this world, and
the best that we find in our travels is an honest friend.

ROBERT LOUIS STEVENSON

*D*iamond mining can be a risky business, with rewards that
are few and far between. Some of the world's largest, most
beautiful diamonds were pulled from the same mine, but de-
cades apart. Why did they keep mining? Why do we keep looking for friends? It is because the promise of that priceless prize
is held out before us.

There is an entire, incredibly complex industry devoted to
unearthing diamonds. For every gem-quality diamond that is
discovered, fourteen *million* times its weight in useless ore has
to be handled. In an average diamond mine, about 250 tons of
ore must be mined to produce a single one-carat polished diamond of gem quality.

> In South Africa, they dig for diamonds. Tons of earth are
> moved to find a little pebble not as large as a little fingernail.
> The miners are looking for the diamonds, not the dirt. They
> are willing to lift all the dirt in order to find the jewels. In
> daily life, people forget this principle and become pessimists
> because there is more dirt than diamonds. When trouble
> comes, don't be frightened by the negatives. Look for the
> positives and dig them out. They are so valuable it doesn't
> matter if you have to handle tons of dirt.
>
> DAVID SEABURY

This obviously does not suggest that the people who aren't
your best friends are dirt. It means that you just need to do a
little sifting to find that someone who is uniquely qualified to
be your friend. Methods of finding friends are just as capricious
and just as arduous as finding diamonds.

When some people go diamond hunting, they come back
heavily laden and are surrounded by dozens of scintillating dis-
coveries. Others are content with one or two priceless jewels.
Do whatever works best for you. But get out there and work at
it, and don't think the work is over just because you found the

right person. A friendship is a dynamic, growing thing and requires continued cultivation.

When I think about my special and close friends and where I found them, I am often amazed. Many of them were found amidst the natural pursuit of my life's chosen profession and passions. There were surprise gifts—diamonds—friendships found in my ordinary work.

The big difference in finding a diamond and in finding a friend is that if you're sincerely looking for a friend it will happen. You can be as sincere as you want in searching for a diamond, but the chances are slim that you will find one. If these happenstance type of situations don't seem to happen to you, and if no amount of digging is turning anything up, don't despair. If there is an individual you're not too sure about, give it some time.

Once you get going, it all comes together. It gains strength from its own momentum. Don't worry over it. There is not one way, perhaps not even a right way. Just look; it's a joyful quest. Whether it's a pebble in a stream or a rock buried beneath tons of ore, it's worth the time and effort.

> Being a friend comes naturally.
> It is taking a moment out of your life
> to give of yourself by bringing comfort,
>   encouragement and peace.
> You do it graciously . . .
>   and I thank you.
>
> LINDA DUPUY MOORE

✦ *A Friend Is Someone Special* ✦

*F*riendship is the feeling you possess for a particular person as distinct from all other persons. It is a very beautiful and intimate and close relationship which is destroyed if it is bestowed casually. To be able to say that you have a friend is to know that there is one person to whom your affairs are as important as his own, on whose aid and counsel and affection you can count on at all times of trouble and distress, to whose aid you will fly the moment you hear he needs your help.

It is impossible for any man or woman to feel like that for more than a few persons.   SAINT JOHN ERVINE

✦ Be a Listener ✦

. . . .

You can make more friends in two months by becoming
interested in other people than you can in two years
by trying to get other people interested in you.

DALE CARNEGIE

I read about a woman in Michigan who created a business out
of listening. Newly divorced, she decided to advertise her offer
to provide a sympathetic ear to the lonely and troubled. The ad
read:

When you need someone to talk to—
24 hours a day.
Call Kathy, Trained Listener, $10.

The first three months she received sixty calls from people
who needed someone to listen to them. Kathy doesn't offer advice, but restricts herself to sympathetic listening.

I think listening is one of the greatest gifts we can give to our
friends. I can't always listen in person or on the phone, but I
listen in letters.

✦ *Be My Friend* ✦

*Y*ou told me you wanted to be my friend
but every time I try to tell you
what is on my heart
you interrupt and tell me
what you think
about what I haven't told you yet.
I am looking for a friend
who can listen sometimes.
Not always
but sometimes.

MARY DELL MILES

✦ *Listen with Your Heart* ✦
. . . .

It is a good and safe rule to sojourn in every place as if you
meant to spend your life there, never omitting an
opportunity of doing a kindness, or speaking
a true word, or making a friend.
JOHN RUSKIN

*O*ne day while giving a seminar in Hawaii, Jim and I had
breakfast with a young dentist and his wife. We were making
small talk and she told me about a beautiful dress she had seen
in the hotel gift shop.

When I asked her if she had bought it she said, "No, I'd love
to but it really is beyond our budget!" and she continued on
explaining the dress in great detail. Small talk. That's all it was.

Later however, as I began speaking to the group, I had an
overwhelming feeling that I should go and try to find the dress
and give it to this woman as a gift.

The left side of my brain kept saying, "But you hardly even
know her name, why should you spend money on a stranger?
Why her and not the others? You can't play favorites." But the
right side of my brain said, "Go and find the dress and get it for
her."

More from emotion than logic, I went to Jim during the next
break and shared my desire. "Go do it," he said, "and I'll fill in
for you at the next session." He gave me the "gift" of his confidence because he didn't ask why I wanted to pursue a desire so
seemingly illogical.

I went to the hotel gift shop and found the dress the woman
had described. The saleslady remembered the woman who had
admired the dress so much, and between the two of us we fig-
ured out what size to get. I purchased the dress, had it gift
wrapped, went back to the hotel, and arranged with the desk
clerk to have the gift put in her room . . . without a gift card or
any indication who the dress was from. Then I returned to the
platform to finish the last session of the seminar.

Later that afternoon, Jim and I were in our room when
someone knocked quietly on our door. We opened the door and
found the woman and her husband standing there.

"Did you have a gift put in my room today?" she asked.

When I admitted it, she asked, "But why? Why would a total stranger bother giving me a gift? You left your speaking session, and the audience who paid to hear you speak, to go to the gift shop and get the dress I casually told you about. Why? I just don't understand."

Both she and her husband had tears rolling down their faces. She poured out her heart to us about how much the act meant to them, not just the dress, but the act of kindness which initiated the gift. She told us that she had been a very stoic person and had great difficulty crying. The gift I gave her was not the dress, but the gift of "tears."

I acted on a quiet urge in my mind even though the logical side of my mind was saying it was foolish. Out of that gift developed the gift of friendship and deep spiritual faith, which had not been theirs before.

✦ *Appreciate Your Friends* ✦

*W*hat a great blessing is a friend . . . with a heart so trusty, you may safely bury your secrets; whose conscience you may fear less than your own; who can relieve your cares by his conversation, your doubts by his counsels, your sadness by his good humor, and whose very looks give you comfort. What a great blessing is a friend.

SENECA

✦ Secondhand Diamonds ✦

It is better to have secondhand diamonds than none at all.

MARK TWAIN

*O*n my fortieth birthday Jim surprised me with an absolutely exquisite diamond ring to replace my original diamond engagement ring. Although I wasn't sure this new ring could ever mean as much to me as my first diamond, I was thrilled to receive this new token of his love.

But what would I do with my old diamond? Eventually I decided to combine it with my mother's diamond in a unique setting. Of all the jewelry I own, this ring is probably the most significant to me—my old diamond and the secondhand diamond from my mother.

The great thing about secondhand diamonds is that they're not like secondhand cars. There are no bad brakes, no dented fenders, no worn-out engines. In fact, sentimental value can increase their worth, at least in our eyes.

Secondhand friends can be more valuable than new ones and are often easier to obtain. They have already been "road-tested" by someone else. Do you and your friends share friends? I heard about a party honoring a woman named Jane who had forty good friends who all knew and liked one another. The one thing they had in common was that they were all introduced to each other by Jane.

Although a friend who is perfectly adapted to you may not hold as much value in another's eyes, being introduced to a friend of a friend is a good way to increase your assets. Meet a friend through a friend, and if the fit is right, the relationship will enrich all involved.

*M*ake new friends, but keep the old;
Those are silver, these are gold.
New-made friendships, like new wine,
Age will mellow and refine.
Friendships that have stood the test—
Time and change—are surely best;
Brow may wrinkle, hair grow gray,
Friendship never knows decay.
For 'mid old friends, tried and true,
Once more we our youth renew.
But old friends, alas! may die,
New friends must their place supply.
Cherish friendships in your breast—
New is good, but old is best;
Make new friends, but keep the old;
Those are silver, these are gold.

JOSEPH PARRY

✦ Acres of Diamonds ✦

Strangers are friends that you have yet to meet.
ROBERTA LIEBERT

*I*n his book *Acres of Diamonds*, Russell Conwell tells the story of Ali Hafed, a wealthy Persian who was quite content with his life until a Buddhist priest visited him and told him about diamonds, explaining that if he owned a mine of diamonds he could do and have anything in the world.

Soon Ali Hafed became quite discontented because he didn't have diamonds. He sold his farm and all his possessions, left his family in the care of a neighbor, and traveled throughout Palestine and Europe looking in vain for a diamond mine. Utterly defeated and broke, he committed suicide in Barcelona, Spain.

One day the same Buddhist priest visited the man who bought Ali Hafed's farm and saw a large stone on the fireplace mantel.

"Has Ali Hafed returned?" he asked. "Here is a diamond!"

"No," said the new owner. "That's just a stone we found in our garden."

It turned out that Ali Hafed's farm, which he sold to search for diamonds, sat on the most magnificent diamond mine in all history, the Golconda. The largest diamonds on earth came from that mine, including the Kohinoor and the Orloff of the crown jewels of England and Russia.

Likewise, our best sources for friendship are often right in our own backyard. The people who know and love us best will often make the best friends.

A nice friendship I discovered in my own backyard developed gradually between Jim's mother and stepfather, Agnes and Bob, and me. They live in a guest house attached to our home. It's nice to go over in the afternoon and have coffee or tea with them. It's a very special time for me to share. It's a time of giving to them but also a time of receiving.

Just as I have become good friends with Jim's parents, so our adult children have become good friends with us. Without realizing exactly when it happened, our children have become our "friends" more than our "kids." This transition has been very meaningful in our lives. We not only still have three children, Beth, Mark, and Katherine, but we have three adult friends who know and love us probably better than anyone else. We have a wonderful history of respect and shared events from past years.

Katherine and Beth and I enjoy doing things together—shopping, walking, laughing, having lunch. I love it when Mark takes me to tea or finds another opportunity for us to be together as friends, not necessarily as mother and son. Another special gift Beth, Mark, and Katherine have given us is the gift of new friends in the form of their spouses, Curt, Melody, and Ken and their families!

But my very best friend is my husband, Jim.

Search the world for friends if you are traveling the world, but don't overlook the gems you have in your own backyard!

✦ *What Is a Friend?* ✦

. . . .

*A*nd what is a friend? Many things . . .

A friend is someone you are comfortable with, someone whose company you prefer. A friend is someone you can count on—not only for support, but for honesty.

A friend is one who believes in you . . . someone with whom you can share your dreams. In fact, a real friend is a person you want to share all of life with—and the sharing doubles the fun.

When you are hurting and you can share your struggle with a friend, it eases the pain. A friend offers you safety and trust, . . . whatever you say will never be used against you.

A friend will laugh with you but not at you . . . a friend is fun.

A friend will pray with you . . . and for you.

My friend is one who hears my cry of pain, who senses my struggle, who shares my lows as well as my highs.

When I am troubled, my friend stands not only by my side, but also stands apart, looking at me with some objectivity. My friend does not always say I am right, because sometimes I am not.

My lover, my friend—this is what a marriage partner should be.

LOU AND COLLEEN EVANS

✦ For Her Eyes Only ✦

One close friend is worth more than
a thousand acquaintances.
UNKNOWN

I know a lady who doesn't believe in friends. Although she has thousands of acquaintances, she thinks her only true friends are family and relatives. Married to a minister, she believes people are only looking for opportunities to criticize her. After a lifetime of being hurt by people she thought were her friends, she closely protects herself and allows no one outside of family to get close.

I want to tell you a story about this lady's attitude toward diamonds. All of her life she worked very hard to stretch her husband's meager salary to provide food and clothing for her family. She was apparently not even capable of dreaming of luxuries until her children were grown and on their own, her husband started receiving an adequate salary, and she started receiving Social Security benefits.

For their fiftieth wedding anniversary she decided she wanted diamonds. Not just one diamond, but lots of diamonds, a ring covered with diamonds. For two years she saved her Social Security checks so she could have a diamond ring for her anniversary. No one in the family was sure their frugal mom could part with her money for this diamond ring, but after months of searching she announced she found her ring, had the money, but was also accepting contributions from the family.

Her family thought she would wear the diamond ring on special occasions. However, it turned out she only wore it around the house for her own enjoyment and hid it when she went to church or to any event where she might see someone she knew. When encouraged by her family to wear it, she replied, "No, if the people at the church see it, they will think we have lots of money and don't need this job."

Although I greatly respect this lady and admire her for the wonderful job she has done raising her family, I would like to tell her that even though friends aren't *necessary* for survival, they give *value* to survival. Like the diamonds purchased for her own enjoyment and whose beauty she doesn't care to share with others, she too has a beautiful radiance that she needs to share with others.

Yes, friends can betray you; but diamonds can be lost, crushed, or stolen. Given a choice between the two, I'll take friends every time.

✦ A Prayer ✦

$God,$
why is it so hard to get close to people,
to let people get close to me, and
to make friends?
Is it because I've been hurt before
and am afraid to be vulnerable again?
Is it because I think
others will take advantage of my openness?
Your Son had twelve close friends.
Yet one sold Him for thirty pieces of silver.
Another denied that he ever knew Him.
The rest ran away
when He needed them most.
Jesus even predicted these things
—yet He didn't shut Himself off
from friendship.
Make me willing to take the risk, too.
Help me to realize that, ultimately, in
opening to another human being
we are opening ourselves to You.
Amen.

UNKNOWN

✦ Pressure Often Makes Diamonds and Friends ✦

> It is better to be in chains with friends
> than in a garden with strangers.
> PERSIAN PROVERB

*D*iamonds are carbon. So is coal. So are we. The differences between the three involve structure, background, pressure, and time. Diamond, with all its inherent properties, is one of the world's simplest compounds. What's unique about a diamond is the way it's put together and the manner in which it was formed. While graphite and coal disintegrate easily and are quite soft, diamond is the hardest naturally occurring substance known. It was formed under a very special set of circumstances. To make it takes one million pounds per square inch of pressure and 3,000 degrees Fahrenheit. Such conditions exist naturally only at a depth 150 miles beneath the surface of the earth.

Have you ever been under so much pressure you felt buried 150 miles beneath the earth? Sometimes friendships are formed when people share that special set of circumstances.

Prisoners of war, hostages, people who've served jury duty or gone to boot camp, and those who've met in the waiting room of an intensive care unit at a hospital know about instant friendships. Out of the severest need and while under intense pressure, a great bond can be formed in an incredibly, unnaturally brief time.

Vietnam veteran Jim Harris described it this way: "Anytime you're in a situation with people you live with very closely, particularly life-threatening situations, you develop friendships and bonds and have memories and a sense of humor perhaps different or unique to the rest of your life's experiences."

Former prisoner of war Everett Alvarez, said, "Acts of self-healing helped us get to know each other through silent conversations across the brick walls . . . learning about each other's childhood, background, experiences, wives and children, hopes and ambitions." The POWs shared poetry, music, the Bible, and their life histories by tapping an alphabet code on the wall or snapping a towel as another POW walked by.

Captain Gerald Coffee said contact with friends kept him

alive for seven years in a concentration camp. Even if it was only a wave, a wink, a tap on the wall, or to have a guy put his thumb up, it made all the difference.

When I heard Captain Coffee speak at the National Speakers' Association meeting, he said that although most of us will never have to suffer like the POWs did, we are all prisoners in one sense or another. Often we are prisoners to our commitments, to our decisions we made years ago, to an unhealthy relationship, and it is what we make out of that experience that determines the kind of people we are in life.

Loretta Girzartis said, "The world is full of lonely people, each isolated in a private, secret dungeon." Many people are in a prison of their own making, feeling lonely, dejected, helpless, trapped, pressured, vulnerable. Friendship is the release that makes it possible to cope. Pressure makes diamonds, but it also makes friends.

✦ Diamond Dust ✦

Adversity is the diamond dust Heaven
polishes its jewels with.
ROBERT LEIGHTON

The wealth of parallels between diamonds and friendship staggers the mind. Consider the diamond: Born in the fires of pressure and adversity, discovered by those in need or want, and cut and shaped by another of its own kind until it is good enough to withstand the test of time. Likewise, the development of a friendship during life's bleaker moments has considerable benefits:

> With the falling of the leaves, the masks of green are stripped off the hillsides, revealing the diversity and uniqueness of each ridge and valley, rock and stream, old shed or oil well hitherto unseen. It is in the winter, when the hills bare their innermost selves, that we get to know them. Then, in the spring, when the masks return, we can look at the hills as old friends few others understand.
>
> So it is with people. Most of the time we wear our masks.

But during the difficult times, during the winters of our lives, we shed our facades and reveal all the intricacies of the unique beings we are. It is in these moments that friendships are formed, and we experience one another as few others ever will.

ANONYMOUS

✦ More Diamond Dust ✦

THE FIRMEST FRIENDSHIPS have been formed in mutual adversity, as iron is most strongly united by the fiercest flame.

CHARLES CALEB COLTON

BE COURTEOUS TO all, but intimate with a few, and let those few be well-tried before you give them your confidence. True friendship is a plant of slow growth, and must withstand the shocks of adversity before it is entitled to the appellation.

GEORGE WASHINGTON

IF A FRIEND of mine . . . gave a feast, and did not invite me to it, I should not mind a bit. . . . But if . . . a friend of mine had a sorrow and refused to allow me to share it, I should feel it most bitterly. If he shut the doors of the house of mourning against me, I would move back again and again and beg to be admitted so that I might share in what I was entitled to share. If he thought me unworthy, unfit to weep with him, I should feel it as the most poignant humiliation.

OSCAR WILDE

✦ Letter from a Friend ✦

. . . .

I am writing to say how much I care for you and that I want you to know me better.

When you awoke this morning I sent a brilliant sunrise through your window hoping to get your attention, but you rushed off without even noticing.

Later I bathed you in warm sunshine and perfumed the air with nature's sweet scent, and still you didn't notice me. As you passed by, I shouted to you in a thunderstorm and painted a beautiful rainbow in the sky and you didn't even look up.

In the evening, I spilled moonlight onto your face and sent a cool breeze to rest you. As you slept, I watched over you and shared your thoughts, but you were unaware that I was so near.

I have chosen you and hope you will talk to me soon. Until then I will remain near. I am your friend and love you very much.   YOUR FATHER IN HEAVEN

. . . .

PART FOUR

Zircons and the Real Thing

. . . .

Types of Friends

✦ Synthetic Gems ✦

PURCHASE NOT FRIENDS by gifts; when thou ceasest to give, such will cease to love.

UNKNOWN

FALSE FRIENDS ARE like migratory birds; they fly away in cold weather.

HASIDIC SAYING

A FRIEND TO all is a friend to none.

ARISTOTLE

THE ANXIETY OF some people to make new friends is so intense that they never have old ones.

ANONYMOUS

THE FELLOW THAT calls you "brother" usually wants something that doesn't belong to him.

KIN HUBBARD

IF WE WOULD build on a sure foundation in friendship, we must love our friends for their sakes rather than for our own.

CHARLOTTE BRONTË

✦ Zircons and the Real Thing ✦

If I were two-faced, would I be wearing this one?

ABRAHAM LINCOLN

People sometimes buy what they think is a diamond and it turns out to be a zircon. We frequently have the same problems with friends. We never really know their value until they are put to the test.

I had a very embarrassing experience with some acquaintances I considered "zircons" but who turned out to be real gems. One night after I spoke, Jim and I had dinner with four couples who attended the seminar. Although we had never met any of them before, they all knew each other and were all from a city thousands of miles away. I had a wonderful conversation with the couple to my left and developed immediate rapport with them to the point that I really avoided getting to know anyone else at the table.

Jim conversed with the couple on his right. We only briefly acknowledged the other couples at the table. Not only was it more difficult to carry on a conversation across the table, but my "friend sensor" eliminated any meaningful relationship with them because they didn't look like the type of people I would be interested in knowing better. After dinner we all exchanged business cards and the couple I had been visiting with extended a cordial invitation for us to stay at their home whenever we were in the area.

I found out later in the week that we would be in the town where these couples lived. We decided we shouldn't pass up the opportunity to develop a friendship with such a great couple. Unable to reach them by phone, we gave our secretary their business card and asked her to send them a telegram notifying them of the time our arrival and letting them know we planned to spend the weekend with them. Thinking everything was under control, we left for another speaking engagement anticipating a wonderful weekend with new friends.

Friday night as we stood outside the airport with our luggage, a car stopped and the couple who sat across the table from us, with whom we had decided there wasn't much possibility for a friendship, got out.

"Sorry we didn't have time to make any advance preparations for your visit, but we just received your telegram today," the wife apologized. "You can have our room. We will sleep on the couch."

It had to be the most embarrassing moment of my life. We had announced our arrival and made demands upon a couple we had hardly even spoken to. Inadvertently we had given the secretary the wrong card and notified the wrong people of our arrival!

Not knowing how best to handle the situation, we said nothing about the mistake. We spent two days and three nights with a couple we had initially screened out as potential friends. However, during those two days and three nights we were treated so kindly and shared with so deeply, we developed two wonderful new friends. These beautiful people were actually honored to have us as their guests (even though they hadn't invited us) and considered it a privilege to get to know us. The privilege was ours.

And the lesson was ours. Once again we had judged people superficially and decided they were "zircons," and not our type. When we became acquainted with them, we found only diamonds.

✦ *Investment-Quality Gems: Real Friends* ✦

YOUR BEST FRIEND is the person who brings out of you the best that is within you.

HENRY FORD

YOUR BEST FRIEND is the one who is a friend without expecting anything.

LEONE DA MODENA

I VALUE THE friend who for me finds time on his calendar, but I cherish the friend who for me does not consult his calendar.

ROBERT BRAULT

FRIENDS LAUGH AT your silliest jokes, put up with your worst moods, go along with your craziest ideas, and always see the best in you.

UNKNOWN

A FRIEND IS someone who understands your past, believes in your future, and accepts you today just the way you are.

UNKNOWN

✦ Industrial-Strength Friends ✦

> The making of friends, who are real friends, is the
> best token we have of a man's success in life.
> EDWARD EVERETT HALE

*T*wo major categories of diamonds are unearthed from the
world's diamond mines—gem quality and industrial quality.
Both are genuine diamonds and are valued for their unique
properties. Over 80 percent of the diamonds in the world are
used industrially. Only 20 percent of those being mined can be
used as gems, and even fewer are large enough to be made into
a jewel much larger than the head of a match.

It's much the same with our friendships—we invest in and
treasure a wide variety of people, but only a small percentage
are our most beloved gems. That small percentage brings us
the greatest reward but we couldn't live without our "industrial" friendships.

While the highest value is associated with gems, industrial
diamonds are much more widespread. Long life, high performance, and precision are the fundamental qualities looked for
in that 80 percent batch of diamonds headed for the rough and
tumble pragmatic usage of industry. Tasks performed range
from the delicate to the mundane, but if it were not for the
unique properties such diamonds possess, much of the industry wouldn't exist.

Diamonds resist acid, penetrate steel, and conduct heat better than any other material. They are unequalled for etching,
grinding, carving, polishing, and sharpening. Copper, brass, and
aluminum are machined by diamond tools, and glass, metals,
ceramics, plastics, carbon, asbestos, and rubber are all pro-
cessed with diamond tools.

Diamond-tipped drill bits are indispensable to the recovery
of oil, while most lenses in glasses have felt the touch of a diamond and contact lens production depends largely on these
stones.

When NASA sent a space probe to Venus in 1978, they
needed a "window" for a camera that could withstand the
planet's corrosive atmosphere and intense heat. Only a diamond would do.

Like industrial-quality diamonds, some friends are valuable for the day-to-day work of life as co-workers, neighbors, or business contacts. Each is unique in his or her own way. We need to accept them as they are rather than try to change them into something they are not.

Throughout a lifetime one meets countless individuals who could become a lifelong friend. Some relationships grow into strong, long-lasting friendships, others are genuine and wonderful during the times you are together but often the situation that brought you together changes as does the friendship. These friendships, though not as captivating or emotionally involving as the very best of gems can be, are nevertheless just as essential as industrial diamonds.

✦ *Heirloom Gems* ✦

I FIND AS I grow older that I love those most whom I loved first.
                                                    THOMAS JEFFERSON

MY COAT AND I live comfortably together. It has assumed all my wrinkles, does not hurt me anywhere, has molded itself on my deformities, and is complacent to all my movements, and I only feel its presence because it keeps me warm. Old coats and old friends are the same thing.
                                                    VICTOR HUGO

WHEN I SEE an honored friend again after years of separation, it is like resuming the words of an old conversation which had been halted momentarily by time. Surely as one gets older, friendship becomes more precious to us, for it affirms the contours of our existence. It is a reservoir of shared experience, of having lived through many things in our brief and mutual moment on earth.
                                                    WILLIE MORRIS
                                                    IN *PARADE*

PART FIVE

Cutting,
Shaping,
and
Polishing

Developing the Relationship

✦ Cutting, Shaping, and Polishing Diamonds ✦

Making friends is the power of going out of one's self. It is
seeing yourself through another's eyes, and, in so doing,
seeing yourself turned from a rough, unhewn
stone into a glittering gem by their
refining, practiced hands.
THOMAS HUGHES

*B*efore the art of diamond-cutting came along, diamonds
were not valued as particularly attractive crystals. In fact, when
the Romans began bringing diamonds from India, they
mounted them for finger rings more for their hardness and
strength than for their beauty. The word *diamond* itself is from
the Greek *adamas,* meaning invincible or unconquered.

Historians think diamond-cutting began in India somewhere
between A.D. 800 and the late 1400s. The art of cutting other
types of gemstones had been around for centuries, but the secret beauty of the diamond had never been revealed. It was
simply too hard and was worn in its natural state. Eventually,
however, somebody tried rubbing one diamond against another. The world has never been the same.

Knowing that diamond cuts diamond is one thing. Actually
forging ahead with the process is something else altogether.
The act of taking a rough stone and turning it into a valuable,
highly prized gem involves six painstaking steps, any of which,
if botched, ruins the diamond.

First, there is marking to determine how it should be cut to
yield the greatest value. After marking with ink, a groove is
cut.

You only get one shot at cleaving. The expert must determine the "grain" of the rough diamond and cut only along the
lines of that grain.

Sawing, the process used to cut across the grain where cleaving is impossible, is a long, precise, and arduous task. A paper-
thin disk only $35/10,000$ of an inch thick, coated with abrasive
diamond dust, digs through the diamond for four to eight
hours.

Girdling is when the diamond is put on a lathe and made
round by the scraping action of even more diamond dust.

The last step is faceting. On a flat wheel of polished iron coated with diamond dust, the emerging gem is given its many facets.

Though the process is not always so deliberate or so well-planned, the same sort of thing happens when we choose a friend or a friend chooses us. At first, we size them up—we look at the rough stone, see the potential, and make a few marks. We may even cut a groove or two.

Next, and only after careful study and when the time and conditions are just right, the major, committing step is taken. It is the point of no return, the point at which friends determine if they can truly adapt to one another. Each gives up something of himself for the sake of pleasing the other, or in other words, one friend—working only along the grain—cleaves the other, and is in turn cleaved by him. If this works out, further shaping and polishing continues virtually as long as the two know each other.

If all this sounds painful, realize that you already know from experience that it isn't torture. You've done this before. Maybe you didn't realize it at the time, but that's what you've been doing all along with the friends you already have.

Making friends is the power of going out of one's self. It is seeing yourself through another's eyes, and, in so doing, seeing yourself turned from a rough, unhewn stone into a glittering gem by their refining, practiced hands.

✦ *You Have Given Me . . .* ✦

*S*trength to know myself
Hope that my life could be better
Kindness when I was hurting
Refuge when I was frightened
Solace for my grief
Faith when I despaired
Options when I felt trapped
Comfort when I was alone
Understanding when I was confused
Challenge for me to change
Patience when I balked
Support when I tried
Acceptance when I failed
Encouragement to go on . . .
Warmth to sustain me
Insight to better comprehend
Knowledge for growth
Recognition of my accomplishments
Guidance toward higher goals
And through all of these,
an example that will sustain
and nurture the person
I am becoming.

                  Thank you for caring.

SHARON CRIST

✦ Polishing Diamonds and Friends ✦

> The gem cannot be polished without friction,
> nor man perfected without trials.
> CHINESE PROVERB

*M*any people are like rough, neglected gems. We live in a world not of strangers, but of undiscovered friends waiting to release their radiance; the craftsmen who do the polishing are that individual's group of loved ones.

The sharpening goes on and on, and it goes both ways. To be a friend, we have to commit to being there for the long haul, ever-ready to engage in the process of cutting, shaping, and polishing.

Just as a diamond is never found pre-cut and ready for the Crown Jewels, friends are seldom ready-made for each other. Some adjusting and affirmation must occur. Of purest necessity, people *must* adapt to one another in order to form a productive relationship. Solomon tells us that "Iron sharpeneth iron; so a man sharpeneth the countenance of his friend." Just as iron sharpens iron, only diamond can cut another diamond. It is this continual contact, this rubbing against one another, that begins the day you make a new friend and continues throughout your relationship with each other.

When iron sharpens iron, both pieces of iron show the wear. In fact, they become mated to one another, and if rubbed together long enough can fit in such a way as to make one believe they were carved out of a larger, solid piece. It can be the same with diamond, and the same with us. Friendship is, indeed, "one of God's best gifts." It is a miracle that renews itself and polishes itself through constant practice, always attaining to the full measure of the beauty one friend sees buried beneath the rough exterior of the other. It is the dynamic, enthralling, and limitlessly rewarding process of life itself.

All friendship is like this, but perhaps none exemplifies it more than marriage. We entered the relationship Naomi Reed and Jim Rhode. We are never 100 percent Reed or Rhode again, but a combination, a sharpened image, hopefully even better people because of the cutting, shaping, and polishing accomplished by our loving friendship.

The same happens in all close friendships. As one who bears the marks of those who have touched my life, I can testify that it is a wonderful experience to be shaped by skilled hands, by the touch of a master. I believe I am a different and infinitely better person because of my close friendships. And certainly this extends also to the deep friendships found in our extended family and even our own children, whose friendship is a precious shaper of qualities in our lives.

✦ *What Is a Friend?* ✦

What is a friend? I will tell you. It is a person with whom you dare to be yourself. Your soul can be naked with him. He seems to ask of you to put on nothing, only to be what you are. He does not want you to be better or worse. When you are with him, you feel as a prisoner feels who has been declared innocent. You do not have to be on your guard. You can say what you think, so long as it is genuinely you. He understands those contradictions in your nature that lead others to misjudge you.

With him you breathe freely. You can avow your little vanities and envies and hates and vicious sparks, your meannesses and absurdities and, in opening them up to him, they are lost, dissolved on the white ocean of his loyalty. He understands. You do not have to be careful.

You can abuse him, neglect him, tolerate him. Best of all, you can keep still with him. It makes no matter. He likes you—he is like fire that purges to the bone. He understands. You can weep with him, sing with him, laugh with him, pray with him. Through it all—and underneath—he sees, knows, and loves you. A friend? What is a friend? Just one, I repeat, with whom you dare to be yourself.

C. RAYMOND BERAN

✦ President of His Fan Club ✦
. . . .

Our opinion of people depends less upon what we see in
them than upon what they make us see in ourselves.
SARAH GRAND

*A*mother and her fifteen-year-old son were discussing his
new girlfriend.

"What does she like about you?" Mom asked.

"That's easy," he said. "She thinks I'm handsome, fun,
smart, and talented."

"What do you like about her?"

"That she thinks I'm handsome, fun, smart, and talented."

How well I remember when each of our children married. I
enjoyed listening to what they loved about their mate and what
their mate loved about our child. They had a way of seeing only
the best in each other and continually praising the other person.

Real friends are like that. They are people who, without res-
ervation, see the best in us and allow us to be ourselves. Real
friends cheer us on and encourage us to attain far beyond what
we believe we are capable of achieving. They are the people
who take a seat in our respective personal and emotional cheering sections. They want to be the president of our fan club.

✦ Your Best Friend ✦
. . . .

MAKE THE MOST of yourself, for that is all there is to you.
UNKNOWN

BETTER KEEP YOURSELF clean and bright; you are the
window through which you must see the world.
GEORGE BERNARD SHAW

FRIENDSHIP IS A special blessing from above. It's the sharing of activities with someone who understands and cares. It's a

warm ray of sunshine that fills our hearts in times of need. It's the bringing out of beautiful things in each other that no one else looked hard enough to find. It's the mutual trust and honesty that lets us be ourselves at all times.

IVERSON WILLIAMS

✦ *Being Your Own Best Friend* ✦

Friendship with oneself is all important because without it one cannot be friends with anyone else in the world.

ELEANOR ROOSEVELT

A friend of mine wears two beautiful diamond rings on her right hand. When I commented on them one day, she said, "They remind me that I have value, to be good to myself, to set goals and make them happen." Then she told me an unusual story about why she had them.

She explained that after seventeen years of marriage they had moved to a new town where her husband took a new job. She had to go to the hospital for a few days to have minor surgery. Her husband said he had to go "out of town on business." When she returned home, she found their bank account and rented home completely cleaned out, her husband and two small children gone without a trace.

Financially depleted, emotionally, mentally, and physically devastated, she ended up sleeping in her car while she looked for work and tried to locate her children and husband. Unable to stop her downward spiral, she realized she had to do something to pull herself back up. One day while walking through a shopping mall applying for jobs at various stores, a beautiful diamond necklace in a jewelry store caught her eye. An almost magnetic attraction to this necklace caused her to return to the store window every day and stare at the brilliance of this diamond.

It was almost as though the sunlight dancing on the diamond was a rainbow of hope promising: "I can belong to you; your life is going to improve; you can pull out of this; don't give up." Finally she walked in the store and asked the price of the necklace and how much it would cost to be made into a ring.

Six months later my friend was wearing the beautiful diamond as a ring. One year later, after locating and obtaining legal custody of her children, she celebrated by giving herself a diamond "pinky" ring to complement the first one. She gives God the credit, but says the beauty of that diamond setting just seemed to encourage her that life could be beautiful again, but she would have to work very hard. She did and it was.

Wearing the rings now is a constant daily reminder of suffering, hard times, and the joy of being thankful for locating her children and finding a wonderful career. She gave them to herself as a gift, but the underlying gift was the renewal of her belief in herself and her value as her own best friend.

Our need for assurance may not be as dramatic as hers and certainly we don't need to buy ourselves diamonds to be our own best friend, but there are many small things we can and should do for ourselves so we can be a friend to others.

BE A FRIEND to yourself, and others will.

SCOTTISH PROVERB

TURN HIM AND see his threads; look if he be
Friend to himself who would be friend to thee.
For that is first requir'd, a man be his own;
But he that's too much that is friend to none.
Then rest, and a friend's value understand,
It is a richer purchase than of land.

BEN JONSON

I DESIRE SO to conduct the affairs of this administration that if at the end, when I come to lay down the reins of power, I have lost every other friend on earth, I shall at least have one friend left, and that friend shall be down inside of me.

ABRAHAM LINCOLN

✦ Diamonds and Friends Can Be Altered ✦

The wise man seeks a friend in whom are those qualities
which he himself may lack; for thus, being united,
is their friendship the more completely
defended against adversity.

JEREMY TAYLOR

*A*lthough the coloring in diamonds occurs naturally, the color can be changed. It was discovered around the turn of the century that a diamond exposed to radium would change color. Bombarding a diamond with a beam of electrons or neutrons "kicks" some of the carbon atoms out of their normal positions, creating new colors—yellow, green, pink, red, or blue.

As diamonds can be altered, so our lives can be altered by our friends. My life is altered by my relationship with my friend and neighbor, Bonnie, with whom I walk endless miles each year. She knows my heart, cares about my family, rejoices in my triumphs, applauds and yet safely assesses my life performance. Bonnie reacts to my ideas and feelings, carefully evaluating what she feels is best for my life.

We don't try to change each other intentionally, but we change each other accidentally by bombarding each other's life, kicking our ideas and thought patterns around until we are altered by the influence of each other. Because of our relationship with each other we become different—experiencing, doing, growing, changing, and learning.

Someone said, "Friends laugh at your silliest jokes, put up with your worst moods, go along with your craziest ideas, and always see the best in you." What is it about your best friend that draws you to him or her? What qualities do they possess that give your life added dimension and fullness?

The manner in which two people connect is different for every friendship because of the uniqueness of the individuals involved. Diamonds generally look colorless because they reflect all wavelengths of visible light equally. But you will display different attributes as you relate to different people. What kind of light do your friends throw on your life? How is it changing you?

✦ Selecting Your Diamonds ✦

THERE ARE FOUR kinds of friendship: friends who will hate your enemies, friends who will fight your battles, friends who will lend you money, and friends who will lend you their ears. It is the latter who suffer the most.   UNKNOWN

THERE ARE THREE friendships which are advantageous: friendship with the upright, with the sincere, and with the man of much observation. Friendship with the man of specious airs, with the insinuatingly soft, and with the glib-tongued, these are injurious.   CONFUCIUS

ON THE CHOICE of friends
Our good or evil name depends.
                    JOHN GAY

. . . .

PART SIX

Sifting Through Diamonds Looking for Dirt

. . . .

Overlooking Flaws

✦ All Diamonds Have Flaws ✦

Diamond miners spend their working lives sifting through
thousands of tons of dirt looking for a few tiny
diamonds. Too often, we do just the opposite
in our intimate friendships. We sift through
the diamonds searching for dirt.

N. STINNETT

*A*ll diamond crystals are impure. Such impurities can adversely affect the properties of the stone, reducing its ability to conduct heat and changing its color. But, sometimes it is precisely these impurities that are most beneficial to a diamond, that create its uniqueness and special beauty. Impurities can stiffen a diamond against permanent deformation under severe stress and can give some of the rarest gems a distinctive color. Flaws may inject bright reds, greens, or blues into a diamond, or they can make the diamond appear cloudy or dirty.

Diamonds grow by adding new carbon atoms to their surfaces. Inclusions, imperfections which are the result of the diamond growing around and trapping a speck of foreign matter, contain much information about the conditions existing at the time the diamond was formed. As the stone grows, the inclusions adapt themselves to the shape of the diamond, becoming very much a part of it. Some diamonds are even famous for their inclusions. The original "Pink Panther" film was supposedly named after a pink, cat-shaped flaw in a diamond that made it unique and valuable.

According to industry standards, a stone can be considered "perfect" if, under the magnification of a 10-power lens, there are no visible flaws, but under greater magnification, no stone is truly flawless. So it is with those you would consider as likely friends. If you look closely enough, you'll be disappointed with everyone. So step back!

Have you discarded a friend for an imperfection, "a piece of dirt," instead of retaining the friendship because of all the diamonds? Or have you ever been discarded for the same reason? On the other hand, a truly blessed, prized friendship is one where we *know* the friend understands, sees, experiences the flaws, and loves intensely anyway. What a gift!

For me, the ultimate in this experience is the complete acceptance I receive from my husband, Jim. After over thirty years of marriage he knows all my flaws but gives me the gift of acceptance and love.

True friendship involves acceptance. The other person accepts us with all our virtues, faults, and peculiarities. Likewise we accept them with all their strengths, weaknesses, and uniqueness.

Accept your friends as you want to be accepted. Take the complete package with strengths and weaknesses and love it for its uniqueness. After all, anyone who looks for a faultless friend will remain friendless, so don't go sifting through diamonds looking for dirt.

✦ *Perfection Is Not Essential to Friendship* ✦

The tide of friendship does not rise high on the banks of perfection. Amiable weaknesses and shortcomings are the food of love. It is from the roughnesses and imperfect breaks in a man that you are able to lay hold of him. . . . My friends are not perfect—no more than I—and so we suit each other admirably. It is one of the charitable dispensations of Providence that perfection is not essential to friendship. ALEXANDER SMITH

✦ Faulty Wiring ✦

I like a friend the better for having
faults that one can talk about.
WILLIAM HAZLITT

I have a very good friend who has a unique "fault" that has popped up a couple of times in our relationship. When he gets behind the wheel of my car, the brake pedal and gas pedal somehow become reversed. Twice he has borrowed my car. Twice he has wrecked my car.

He felt terrible when he smashed my car a few years ago. We had all but forgotten it until he recently borrowed my car again to do *me* a favor. Somehow in the five-minute time period between the time I gave him the keys and the time he arrived to pick me up, he smashed in the side of my car.

No words could adequately express what either one of us was feeling. He was terribly embarrassed and I found humor in the helpless, little-boy look on his face. Unable to speak a word, I collapsed in laughter until tears rolled down my face. He was near tears himself, but not because he saw the humor of the event. What I saw as hilarious, he saw as a thousand-dollar payment. When he needed sympathy and understanding, all I could offer him was laughter. I did not criticize him for the damage to my car; he did not criticize me for my laughter. I can easily accept him despite his occasional flaws because he so lovingly accepts me despite mine.

✦ Faults Are Part of Our Sparkle ✦

LOVE IS BLIND; friendship closes its eyes.

FRENCH PROVERB

IT IS WELL, when one is judging a friend, to remember that he is judging you with the same godlike and superior impartiality.

ARNOLD BENNETT

ALL WE CAN do is to make the best of our friends, love and cherish what is good in them, and keep out of the way of what is bad.

THOMAS JEFFERSON

. . . I HAVE NEVER made an acquaintance since that lasted, or a friendship that lasted with any that had not some tincture of the absurd in their characters. . . . I venerate an honest obligation of understanding. The more laughable blunders a man shall commit in your company, the more tests he giveth you that he will not betray or overreach you.

CHARLES LAMB

✦ Disposable Diamonds ✦

Every friend has at least one flaw. I'm sure I have more
than one. Friendship has got to be accepting, forgetful
of what isn't perfect because of all that is. People
who don't go along with that run the risk of
losing something very precious.
It would be like throwing a diamond in the trash because
you discover it has one tiny flaw. Worse than that.
You can always pick up a new diamond at the
jeweler's, but you can never replace a friend.

GAYLE LAWRENCE

*H*ave you ever known anyone who threw away a diamond?
As unlikely as it sounds, some people throw away their dia-

monds when they tire of the relationship the diamond symbolizes. For a few people, that doesn't take too long.

I heard of a couple who, on their wedding night, went out to dinner with the best man and matron of honor. The groom said something the bride didn't like and she threw one of her first in what became an ongoing series of temper tantrums. Rage overtook reason as she took off her diamond and threw it across the restaurant.

Horrified, the groom and the best man spent the next forty-five minutes on their hands and knees looking for the discarded diamond, a precious heirloom that had belonged to his mother. Apparently the bride decided to throw away the diamond because her new husband had a flaw. Eventually the bride's flaws caused her to lose something far more precious than the diamond—her husband.

✦ *Overlooking Flaws* ✦

MY FRIEND IS he who will tell me my faults, in private.

IBN GABIROL
CHOICE OF PEARLS

IT IS ONE of the severest tests of friendship to tell your friend his faults. So to love a man that you cannot bear to see a strain upon him, and to speak painful truth through loving words, that is friendship.   HENRY WARD BEECHER

TWO PERSONS CANNOT long be friends if they cannot forgive each other's little failings.   UNKNOWN

WHO SEEKS A friend without a fault remains without one.

TURKISH PROVERB

PART SEVEN

Caring for Our Diamonds

Preventing Broken Friendships

✦ Caring for Your Diamonds ✦

A man should keep his friendships in constant repair.
SAMUEL JOHNSON

*F*or seventeen years I left my mother's diamond in a safe-deposit box rather than wearing it as a daily reminder of her. Now I wear it almost every day and am constantly reminded of the beauty of her life. All too often our friendships are exactly like diamonds. Polished, cared for, and treated gingerly, held in our hands for only moments at a time then safely stored away again, they provide us with pleasure whenever it's convenient. The rest of the time we keep our friends in the "safe-deposit boxes" of our minds rather than enjoying their beauty on a daily basis.

Such relationships are not truly dynamic and growing. They frequently bear all the cold, hard, impersonal, and materialistic properties that can leave diamond ownership a valueless experience.

Diamonds, as hard as they are, are not indestructible. They can be shattered by a small blow if it is in the right place. As a friend, it is your duty to protect the vulnerabilities of those you love. Your friends may have seen you through thick and thin, and endured great hardships with you, but if you hit them where it hurts, you could shatter the relationship forever. Henry Ward Beecher said, "It is one of the severest tests of friendship to tell your friend his faults. So to love a man that you cannot bear to see a strain upon him, and to speak painful truth through loving words, that is friendship."

Great care is required to discover perfect gems and even greater care is entrusted to the one who keeps the gem. To keep them looking their best they need to be cleaned, polished, and have the setting checked on a regular basis. Friendship is the same way.

Considering all the time some people spend cleaning, polishing, shining, admiring, and safely storing a rock, it is amazing the number of human relationships that are left to be covered with dust and dirt and later lost due to neglect.

✦ The Art of Friendship ✦

𝓕riendship is the art of forgetting oneself totally, all selfish needs and wants, and getting to know the person and character of one another.

It's learning to accept a person not for what they are on the outside, but for what they reveal to you from the inside. It's strengthening oneself with the qualities found in a friend and the experiences shared with each other.

It's learning and growing to care for a person in such a way that you hurt when they hurt, and you are able to feel their joy when it comes to them.

Friendship means being there to give to one another without any thought of taking, being there to support another when they are weak, or giving them your smile when they have lost their own.

Friendship is the blending of two unique souls to form a complete spirit with a common bond of love and caring. The art of friendship, in its most basic form, is love that cares.

VICKI MCCLELLAND JETER

✦ Come Share My Lap with Me ✦

A friend is someone who sings with you when you are
on the mountain top and silently walks beside
you through the valley.
UNKNOWN

𝓢arah was only seven years old when Sandy, her next door neighbor and best friend, was killed in a freak accident. Sarah told her mother she needed to go see Sandy's mother and make her feel better.

When she returned home, Sarah's mother asked her what she had done to comfort Sandy's mother.

With lower lip quivering, Sarah replied, "I just sat on her lap and cried with her."

THE TRUE TEST of friendship is to be able to sit or walk with a friend for an hour in perfect silence without wearying of one another's company.   DINAH MARIA MULOCK CRAIK

THAT FRIENDSHIP ONLY is indeed genuine when two friends, without speaking a word to each other, can nevertheless find happiness in being together.   GEORGE EBERS

IF YOU HAVE a friend worth loving, love him. Yes, and let him know that you love him ere life's evening tinge his brow with sunset glow. Why should good words ne'er be said of a friend—till he is dead?   UNKNOWN

WE HAVE A generation of people who are working terribly hard to find things to do together, thinking that friendship comes out of that kind of frenetic activity . . . the sort of carousing good fellowship you see on television beer commercials. There's nothing wrong with that, but it is not friendship.

The real test of friendship is: Can you literally do nothing with the other person? Can you enjoy together those moments of life that are utterly simple? They are the moments that people look back on at the end of life and number as the most sacred experiences they've ever had.   EUGENE KENNEDY

YOU CANNOT ALWAYS cure, but you can always comfort.
HIPPOCRATES, 460 B.C.

✦ An Example of Friendship ✦
. . . .

One example of friendship remains with me as vividly as the moment I first heard of it as a boy. In his first season with the Brooklyn Dodgers, Jackie Robinson, the first black man to play major league baseball, faced venom nearly everywhere he traveled—fastballs at his head, spikings on the bases, brutal epithets from the opposing dugouts and from the crowds. During one game in Boston, the taunts and racial slurs seemed to reach a peak. In the midst of this, another Dodger, a southern white man named Pee Wee Reese, called time-out. He walked from his position as shortstop toward Robinson at second base, put his arm around Robinson's shoulder, and stood there with him for what seemed like a long time. The gesture spoke more eloquently than the words: This man is my friend.

WILLIE MORRIS
IN *PARADE MAGAZINE*

✦ *The Only Way to Have a Friend* ✦

$\mathcal{T}$he only way to have a friend
  Is to be one yourself;
The only way to keep a friend
  Is to give from that wealth.

For friendship must be doublefold,
  Each one must give his share
Of feelings true if he would reap
  The blessings that are there.

If you would say, "He is my friend,"
  then nothing else will do
But you must say, "I am his friend,"
  And prove that fact be true.

AUTHOR UNKNOWN

✦ *Alabaster Boxes* ✦

. . . .

*D*o not keep the alabaster boxes of your love and tenderness sealed up until your friends are dead. Fill their lives with sweetness. Speak approving, cheering words while their ears can hear and while their hearts can be thrilled and made happier by them. Say the kind things you mean to say to them before they go. The flowers you mean to send should brighten and sweeten your friends' homes before they leave. If my friends have alabaster boxes laid away, full of fragrant perfumes of sympathy and affection, I would rather they bring them out in my weary and troubled hours and open them, that I may be refreshed and cheered. Let us learn to anoint our friends beforehand. Post-mortem kindnesses do not cheer the burdened spirit. Flowers cast no fragrance backward over the weary way.

UNKNOWN

*A*round the corner I have a friend,
In this great city that has no end;
Yet days go by, and weeks rush on,
And before I know it a year is gone,
And I never see my old friend's face,
For Life is a swift and terrible race.
He knows I like him just as well
As in the days when I rang his bell
And he rang mine. We were younger then,
And now we are busy, tired men:
Tired with playing a foolish game,
Tired with trying to make a name.
"Tomorrow," I say, "I will call on Jim,
Just to show that I'm thinking of him."
But tomorrow comes—and tomorrow goes,
And the distance between us grows and grows
Around the corner!—yet miles away . . .
"Here's a telegram, sir . . ."

                     "Jim died today."
And that's what we get, and deserve in the end:
Around the corner, a vanished friend.

CHARLES HANSON TOWNE

✦ *Epitaph for a Friend* ✦

"Here lies the friend of Sir Philip Sydney."
(ORDERED BY LORD BROOKE TO BE
ENGRAVED UPON HIS OWN
TOMBSTONE.)

*R*eal friendships are marked by devotion to one another. I discovered one friendship while touring Andrew Jackson's home in Tennessee. Jackson had a slave who was born on his plantation, lived there all his life, and died at the age of ninety-nine. Throughout his life, this wonderful black man loved Andrew Jackson and was committed to him. His only dying request was that he be buried next to his best friend, Andrew Jackson. As you go out into the family graveyard, amidst all the impressive tombstones, there is a small rock next to Jackson's grave marking the grave of his slave and affirming the value of the friendship.

Do not save your loving speeches
For your friends till they are dead;
Do not write them on their tombstones,
Speak them rather now instead.

ANNA CUMMINS

✦ *The Best Thing in Life Is a Friend* ✦

*O*ne of the best things about life is friends. You find them wherever you go.

Friends are essential because they help bring out the best in you. When they see your worst, they still care. They just accept.

Friends are the stars in your happy memories. In your sad memories, they are the shoulders you leaned on and the hearts that listened. They just care.

Friends help you in your times of need. When things are going smoothly, they are content to be your friend. They just know.

Friends help create all your fun times, always there to spread laughter and joy. When you need tears, friends provide these, too. They just understand.

You, my friend, are all of these. And most of all, when you need it, remember friends just love, as I do you.

MARIA ELENA NAJERA

. . . .

PART EIGHT

Why Diamonds Break

. . . .

and Friends Drift Apart

✦ Shattering Diamonds ✦

> Friendship is a vase, which, when it is flawed by heat, or
> violence, or accident, may as well be broken at once; it
> can never be trusted after. . . . Coarse stones, if
> they are fractured, may be cemented
> again; precious ones never.
> WALTER SAVAGE LANDOR

A doctor in Los Angeles became distraught when his former girlfriend announced plans to marry another man. He yanked the new two-carat diamond ring, given to her by the man she planned to marry, from her finger, went down to his basement, and crushed it in a vise. The new suitor called officers after learning the $10,000 diamond had been destroyed and police booked the doctor for investigation of robbery.

Diamonds are the hardest gemstone known to man but they are not indestructible. As precious and beautiful as they are, they are crystalline and inflexible and can only take so much stress. They have a melting point of 6,900 degrees Fahrenheit—two and a half times higher than that of steel—and will ultimately burn and convert into carbon monoxide and carbon dioxide. If hit in the wrong place, a diamond can easily be shattered into dust. Diamonds, tough as they are, cannot absorb a shock; friends must.

Exposed to the rigors of real life and day-to-day turmoil, the bonds that compose some friendships can be smashed just as easily as a diamond. The closer and more precious the friendship becomes, the more carefully we must guard it from devastating influences.

As a friend, it is your duty to protect the vulnerabilities of those you love. Your friends may have seen you through good and bad or happy and sad times and endured great hardships with you, but if you hit them where they are vulnerable, you could shatter the relationship forever. The closer the friend, the more we know and the more deeply we can hurt through our words, actions, or revelations. What a holy trust is this thing called deep friendship!

While the bonds of friendship must be as strong as the links which hold the carbon molecules of a diamond together, friends must flex and bend when necessary. With this added measure of strength and resiliency, real friendship is infinitely more valuable and more beautiful than any diamond.

✦ *Preventing Broken Friendships* ✦

THE BEST WAY to keep friendships from breaking is not to drop them.

UNKNOWN

A FRIEND MUST not be injured, even in jest.

SYRUS

THE LANGUAGE OF friendship is not words, but meanings. It is an intelligence above language.

HENRY DAVID THOREAU

THERE ARE MANY moments in friendship, as in love, when silence is beyond words. The faults of our friend may be clear to us, but it is well to seem to shut our eyes to them.

Friendship is usually treated by the majority of mankind as a tough and everlasting thing which will survive all manner of bad treatment. But this is an exceedingly great and foolish error; it may die in an hour of a single unwise word. . . .

MARIE LOUISE DE LA RAMEE

DON'T FLATTER YOURSELF that friendship authorizes you to say disagreeable things to your intimates. The nearer you come into relation with a person, the more necessary do tact and courtesy become.

OLIVER WENDELL HOLMES

✦ *Distance Often Separates Friends* ✦

I HAVE LOST friends, some by death—others through sheer inability to cross the street. VIRGINIA WOOLF

GO OFTEN TO the house of thy friend for weeds choke up the unused path. UNKNOWN

WE TAKE CARE of our health, we lay up money, we make our room tight, and our clothing sufficient; but who provides wisely that he shall not be wanting in the best property of all— friends? RALPH WALDO EMERSON

AFFECTION CAN WITHSTAND very severe storms of vigor, but not a long polar frost of indifference.

SIR WALTER SCOTT

FRIENDSHIP, LIKE LOVE, is destroyed by long absence, though it may be increased by short intermissions.

SAMUEL JOHNSON

WHEN WE LIVED near each other we participated in the same activities. Our friendship was strong because we shared so many things. Now—living apart we rarely see each other but our friendship is even stronger because we share the same feelings. This closeness of hearts is what makes a lifetime friendship like ours.

SUSAN POLIS SCHUTZ

NO DISTANCE OF place or lapse of time can lessen the friendship of those who are thoroughly persuaded of each other's worth.

ROBERT SOUTHEY

FRIENDS, NO MATTER how far separated, will grow in love and sympathy and nearness to each other.

UNKNOWN

✦ *Fate Smiled on One but Not the Other* ✦

A TRUE FRIEND is one who likes you in spite of your achievements.
UNKNOWN

IF AT FIRST you don't succeed, you'll probably have more friends.
UNKNOWN

TAKE ENVY OUT of a character and it leaves greater possibilities for friendships.
ELIZABETH B. CUSTER

HE WHO GIVES up a friendship for ambition burns a picture to obtain the ashes.
ARABIC PROVERB

✦ *Money Reared Its Ugly Head* ✦

THE MAN WHO has no money to lend friends makes no enemies.
UNKNOWN

THE HOLY PASSION of Friendship is of so sweet and steady and loyal and enduring a nature that it will last through a whole lifetime, if not asked to lend money.
MARK TWAIN

BEFORE BORROWING MONEY from a friend decide which you need most.
AMERICAN PROVERB

WHEN A FRIEND deals with a friend, let the bargain be clear and well penn'd, that they may continue friends to the end.
BENJAMIN FRANKLIN

FRIENDSHIP IS LIKE money, easier made than kept.

SAMUEL BUTLER

✦ *One of Us Was Overly Sensitive* ✦

*A*nd Heaven protect us also from the easily offended friend who, refusing to understand once and for all that we are fond of him but that life is short and difficult and human beings capricious, watches us unceasingly so that he may interpret every manifestation of impatience or bad humor as an omen. An easily offended person will never make real friends. True friendship implies full confidence, which may only be completely given or completely withdrawn. If friendship has continually to be analyzed, nursed, and cured, it will cause more anguish than love itself, without having love's strength and its remedies.

ANDRE MAUROIS

PROMISES MAY GET thee friends, but non-performance will turn them into enemies.   UNKNOWN

BE SLOW IN choosing a friend, slower in changing.
                                      BENJAMIN FRANKLIN

KEEP WELL THY tongue and keep Thy friends.
                                      GEOFFREY CHAUCER

WE MAKE MORE enemies by what we say than friends by what we do.   JOHN CHURTON COLLINS

THE BEST WAY to keep your friends is not to give them away.
                                      WILSON MIZNER

✦ Friends May Have Conflicting Values ✦

I NEVER CONSIDERED a difference of opinion in politics, in religion, in philosophy, as cause for withdrawing from a friend.

THOMAS JEFFERSON

A FOE TO God was ne'er true friend to man,
Some sinister intent taints all he does.

EDWARD YOUNG
NIGHT THOUGHTS

SENTIMENTS ARE WHAT unites people, opinions what separates them. Sentiments are a simple bond that gathers us together; opinions represent the principle of variety that scatters. The friendships of youth are founded on the former, the cliques of old age are to be blamed on the latter. If we could only realize this early and arrive at a liberal view as regards others in cultivating our own attitude of mind, we would be more conciliatory and try to collect by the bond of sentiment what opinion has dispersed.

JOHANN WOLFGANG VON GOETHE

✦ Some Diamonds Come with a Curse ✦

The cruise ship reached warm Jamaican waters and it was the night when dinner meant formal dress. At one end of the table, a man noticed the woman next to him was wearing a diamond pendant. It was just about the biggest diamond he had ever seen.

"I hope you don't mind my saying so, but that diamond is beautiful," he said.

She smiled pleasantly.

"I don't mind at all, and thank you," she said. "It's the Klopman diamond."

The guy looked puzzled.

"I've heard of the Hope diamond and some others," he said, "but the Klopman is a new one to me."

The woman explained the Klopman diamond was much like the Hope diamond, though somewhat smaller. However, the cut was identical and it was equal in quality. The Klopman even came with a curse, the same as the Hope diamond.

"That's astonishing, and it comes with a curse?" the man asked.

The woman nodded.

"If you'll forgive my curiosity, what kind of a curse?" he asked.

"Mr. Klopman."

ALEX THIEN
MILWAUKEE SENTINEL

✦ Diamonds You Don't Want to Own ✦

Better one friend with a dish of food
than a hundred with a gripe.
UNKNOWN

*D*iamonds are exquisite, shimmering, light-filled rocks from the earth. Battles have been fought over them; people have killed for them; some have paid millions of dollars to own them; thieves have risked their lives to steal them. Yet, for all their value and beauty, these incredible gems have often brought people misery.

Those who've been associated with the legendary cursed diamonds of history have paid a high price for their infatuation. In 1701 a destitute native miner in India discovered a large gem. He tried to sell it to a sea captain who insisted the miner come on a journey resulting in the miner being thrown overboard. The captain sold the diamond for a modest sum and eventually hanged himself. Later it was sold to Thomas Pitt, who became suspicious and slept with the diamond under his pillow and a gun by the bed. Later it was sold to the French royal family and supposedly caused Louis XVI to lose his head on the guillotine. The diamond, known as the Regent, now resides in the Louvre museum where it is no longer causing anyone any harm.

Another diamond with a horrible history is the Hope Diamond now on display in the Smithsonian Institute. Rumors about the stone being stolen from the right eye of a statue of an Indian god led to the belief that the god cursed the stone resulting in the tragic deaths of those who owned the diamond.

Some think the misfortunes that befell people who came under the spell of the diamond were mixtures of coincidence and superstition. Others believe diamonds can be as unlucky as they are beautiful. It is hard to look past the beauty of a diamond and see the problems that might lurk in the future. Friendship is much the same. A newfound "gem" can be very beautiful and appealing and it can be very difficult to know how destructive it could be to your life.

Jim and I once socialized with a couple who fought and argued all the time. One night our kids asked, "Why are you

always in such a bad mood after you go out with those people?''
Our kids made us realize these friends were dragging us down
emotionally.

Some "friends" overlook the beauty and grandeur of you as
a person and concentrate on your flaws. They may violate con-
fidences, make light of things which are serious to you, put you
down, and forget commitments. You may have had great times
with them, but frequently they lack the ability to support and
care for you. There comes a time when you have to pull away
from these people. If they won't go away, get away.

My desire and love of friendship, my belief in people, and
my excitement in exploring the depths of persons make me
want to believe that there are no friends you wouldn't want. It
has been a painful journey to discover otherwise.

NEVER BREAK OFF the friendship, rather untie it, when those you become bound to appear cheats.   JAMES PUCKLE

AN OPEN FOE may prove a curse;
But a pretended Friend is worse.
BENJAMIN FRANKLIN

BECAUSE DISCRETION IS always predominant in true friendship, it works and prevails least upon fools. Wicked men are often reformed by it, weak men seldom.

EDWARD HYDE, LORD CLARENDON

TO BE INTIMATE with a foolish friend is like going to bed with a razor.   UNKNOWN

WE OUGHT TO flee the friendship of the wicked, and the enmity of the good.   EPICTETUS

*E*very friendship that lasts is built of certain durable materials. The first of these is truthfulness. If I can look into the eyes of my friend and speak out always the truthful thought and feeling with the simplicity of a little child, there will be a real friendship between us.   BERTHA CONDE

PART NINE

Finding
Lost
Diamonds

. . . .

Restoring Friendships

✦ The "Sewer Brigade" ✦

> It is delightful to me to go mad
> over a friend restored to me.
>
> HORACE

I recently read an article in the paper about a newlywed who accidentally flushed her $1,800 diamond wedding ring down the toilet. Her husband, who was still making payments on the ring, wasn't going to let the one-carat diamond get away without a fight. He spent the night digging up the yard and tearing up the plumbing searching for the ring.

The wife spent the night at her sister's house because "he was really upset and I didn't want to be around him."

By morning the frustrated groom felt the ring was no longer in the plumbing in his house, so he called the water department. The city sent out its "lost diamond crew" to look for the tiny, valuable rock.

After installing a trap at a downstream manhole, they flushed the pipe by sending a high pressure stream of water down the sewer pipe. Then one of the crew crawled down into the manhole and fished the diamond ring out of the sewage.

Just about any relationship is worth restoring. But we have to take action. How far are you willing to go to refind a lost relationship?

✦ Waiting for the Tide to Come In ✦

> To lose an old friend is as the loss of a bead from
> life's rosary; or to drop a jewel into the
> depths of a turbulent sea.
> DOUGLAS MEADER

*F*ortunately, I have not had to look in the sewer for any of my diamonds, but I have had to carefully search airplanes and motel rooms until I found diamonds that had fallen out of my jewelry. Even though insurance covers the cost of replacing lost diamonds, nothing can replace the sentimental value of a particular gem—or a lost friend.

On one particular trip to Maui I lost two diamonds. My initial response when I first noticed a diamond was missing from one of my rings was "it's gone." It seemed hopeless that I would ever find it. Jim's attitude was more positive than mine and he began searching the carpet of our room. Finally, after taking apart the plumbing he found it in the trap of the bathroom sink.

Later on that same trip, I was by myself flying to a seminar and I noticed a little diamond from my watch was gone. This time, rather than giving up, I decided to look for it. I carefully felt all around me and eventually found it on the seat next to me. Afraid that I would lose it in the deep velour, I asked a stewardess for some scotch tape and used the tape to pick up the diamond. I rolled the tape around it so I wouldn't lose it again before I got a chance to put it back.

In both incidents the holes that were left when the diamonds were missing seemed much larger than I expected. The diamonds themselves didn't seem that large, but the difference their absence made shocked me.

You may not realize how important a friend is until he or she is gone, leaving an ugly, gaping hole in your life. Some just say "he or she is gone," while others make lifelong attempts to restore the relationship.

I have a broken friendship which I have never given up wanting or hoping to restore. After years of praying and hoping, I am at peace with the eventual outcome. But that peace does not negate the fact that a large hole has been left in my life by the absence of this relationship.

On the other hand, a "gem" of a relationship recently came back to me. It is as if we had never been separated, except for the sadness of the wasted years. How infinitely precious is the gift of a returned relationship, a found diamond.

QUARREL WITH A friend and you're both wrong.

LAO-TZU

OUTWITTED

HE DREW A circle that shut me out—
Heretic, rebel, a thing to flout.
But Love and I had the wit to win:
We drew a circle that took him in!

EDWIN MARKHAM

FRANK EXPLANATIONS WITH friends in case of affronts sometimes save a perishing friendship; sometimes they even place it on a firmer basis than before. Secret discontent always ends badly. And by the way, we ought to remember that the word *friendship* applies to relations in the family quite as much as with outsiders. Somebody once said that love may not be any part of friendship but friendship must always exist for love to be happy.

SYDNEY SMITH

✦ Suspect Told to Cough Up Diamonds ✦

> To our friends, who know the worst
> about us but refuse to believe it.
> TOAST TO FRIENDS

*W*hen police responded to a report of a break-in at a house in Wilkinsburg, Pennsylvania, they detained the suspect while the homeowner inventoried his possessions. After determining that a .32 caliber revolver and two diamond rings were missing, the police obtained a search warrant.

A preliminary search of the suspect uncovered the revolver, but the diamonds were not to be found. Convinced that the diamonds were in his possession, police took the suspect to the hospital where x-rays revealed two diamonds rings in his stomach.

Four options existed for recovering the rings, none of them very pleasant, but the "suspect," now termed "burglar," agreed to the least painful one and coughed up the diamonds.

What does this story have to do with friendships? Maybe nothing; maybe a lot, depending on your perspective. Our friends function like x-rays in our lives. Real friends can see through us. Not only can they see the diamonds others don't see, but they understand us and often see things in our lives that we don't want to admit. Sometimes they overlook it and let it pass. Other times they confront us—or carefront us, as I prefer to say—and make us deal with something that needs to be faced.

✦ *Funeral Etiquette* ✦

EVERY MAN SHOULD keep a fair-sized cemetery in which to bury the faults of his friends.
H. W. BEECHER

WHEN TWO FRIENDS part they should lock up each other's secrets and exchange keys. The truly noble mind has no resentments.
DIOGENES

DO NOT CONDEMN your friend: you do not know what you would have done in his place.
HILLEL

SUPPOSE ONE'S FRIENDS may be right till one finds them wrong; rather than to suppose them wrong till one finds them right.
BENJAMIN FRANKLIN

✦ *Epitaph for a Friendship* ✦

To bury a friendship is a keener grief
than to bury a friend.
HUGH BLACK

There's hardly anything that hurts more than the breakdown of a relationship. To lose a friend to death is one thing. We grieve and learn to put the hurt behind us. To lose a friend because of a shattered relationship is quite another matter—it is a kind of living death from which there seems to be no release. I believe that when we lose a friendship we die a little.

When a friend dies, we are comforted by our memories of the good times we had with that friend. It should be the same way when we lose a friendship. Do everything possible to restore the relationship, but until that happens, think about the good and happy times. Concentrate on the positive; dwell on the good; be grateful for the wonderful days, weeks, months, or years you had together. Don't let the negative side overpower your gratitude for the positive side.

Until the relationship is restored, which sometimes might take years, be even more careful what you say about the person. Never give up hope of restoring the relationship. Just about any relationship is worth restoring, but we have to take action.

A friend is someone who listens without judging you right or wrong, good or bad, and gently helps you define your thoughts to regain perspective.

When you're feeling bad about yourself, a friend is there to remind you of all those positive qualities you may have forgotten.

When you share with a friend, decision-making becomes easier and problems seem less critical.

A friend gives you the priceless gift of time: time to share, to try out new ideas and rethink old ones. No matter how often you're together, you discover dimensions of yourself through the bonds and the mirror of friendship.

A friend loves you for who you are, not what you do. Feeling so accepted, you are able to set higher goals, try harder, and achieve more.

Through close friendship, you learn the fine art of giving. You expand, become more selfless, feel more deeply, and help more effectively. Seeing the happiness you bring to another person gives you a greater sense of well-being and increases your capacity to love.

Wherever you go in life, whatever stage or place you reach, a friend who has entered your soul is always with you, gently guiding, faithfully following, and ever walking beside you.

SANDRA STURTZ

PART TEN

A
Special
Gem

The Friend of Friends

✦ *A Special Friend* ✦
. . . .

*D*id you ever think about God as your friend? As someone who is totally involved in your life? Someone who wants to give you the best there is, a share in His eternal happiness?

"No longer do I call you servants . . . ," Jesus told His disciples, "but I have called you friends."

God comes to us in the Person of Jesus to tell us He is our Friend. He asks us to enter a close relationship with Him. He wants us to enjoy His presence as we enjoy the company of a special Friend.

He knows how in our humanity we struggle, make mistakes, become discouraged. How we need forgiveness, comfort, and strength. How we need His help to grow in spirit. He gives it through many sources. One is human friendship.

JOSEPH R. THOMAS

✦ The Essence of a Good Friend ✦

Ointment and perfume rejoice the heart; so doth the
sweetness of a man's friend that cometh of
hearty counsel. Thine own friend and
thy father's friend forsake not.

SOLOMON

*A*number of years ago I received a very special birthday
gift from Jim. He took me to Scottsdale for an appointment
with a perfumer named Erné who has been in the perfume
business for most of his life and was the creator of several classic
perfumes. He custom creates scents to suit the personality and
unique characteristics of each client.

This master of his craft interviews each client for about an
hour in order to create a special perfume representative of
them. Part of the fun is that each person gets to name their
fragrance. Jim named my fragrance "My Sweetness" because
that is one of the meanings of my name, Naomi. It was an incredible experience.

Because I enjoyed it so much, I have given this experience as
a gift to many friends through the years. However, it was especially fun and rewarding when I gave the gift to one particular
friend. She grew up in Belgium and has an artistic nature. She
talked about a childhood memory of the smell of beautiful
white flowers in the mountains surrounding her home.

Erné chose to create a very lovely, light scent for her and she
named it "Symphony Blanche," which means "white symphony." It was perfect for her. And mine is perfect for me. In
fact, whenever I wear it, Jim recognizes it immediately.

Erné has hundreds of bottles of fragrance components from
which he carefully selects portions. He blends them on a blotter
strip and allows each client to smell each ingredient as it is
added. He continues to mix them together until he finally
reaches the perfect blend to meet the customer's satisfaction.

Certainly we can have a fragrance created for us—and that is
fun. But whether or not we have Erné do it, *we have* created a
fragrance, an essence, an aroma all our own. The fragrance of
our life is the difference we make in a room when we enter it

and the memory we leave behind. We each have a very unique fragrance—hopefully one that blesses others by our presence.

I love the story in the Bible about the woman who broke an alabaster jar and poured perfume on Christ's head. It was expensive and people rebuked her. Christ responded, "She did what she could. . . . I tell you the truth, wherever the gospel is preached throughout the world, what she has done will also be told, in memory of her." Her actions left a fragrance that has lasted through centuries.

Let us pray that the fragrance of our lives will fill the lives of others with God's essence—a fragrance of sweetness, kindness, tolerance, understanding, forgiveness, fairness, and godliness.

✦ Broken and Spilled Out ✦

One day a plain village woman
Driven by love for her Lord
Recklessly poured out a valuable essence
Disregarding the scorn.

And once it was broken and spilled out
A fragrance filled all the room
Like a pris'ner released from his shackles
Like a spirit set free from the tomb.

Broken and spilled out
Just for love of you Jesus
My precious treasure
Lavished on Thee.

Broken and spilled out
And poured at your feet
In sweet abandon, let me be
Spilled out and used up for Thee.

Lord, you were God's precious treasure
His loved and His own perfect Son
Sent here to show me the love of the Father
Just for love it was done.

And though you were perfect and holy
You gave up yourself willingly
You spared no expense for my pardon
You were used up and wasted for me.

Broken and spilled out
Just for love of me Jesus
God's most precious treasure,
Lavished on me.

Broken and spilled out
And poured at my feet,
In sweet abandon, Lord you
Were spilled out and used up for me.

In sweet abandon, Lord, you were
Spilled out and used up for me.

Words by Gloria Gaither and Bill George. © 1984 Gaither Music Co. and Yellow House Music. All rights reserved. Used by permission.

✦ Diamonds and Friends Reflect Light ✦

A diamond is a congealed drop of sunlight . . . literally
and scientifically . . . a diamond is an actual
deposit of carbon from the sun. . . .
RUSSELL H. CONWELL
ACRES OF DIAMONDS

*I*n their rough, natural state, diamonds can be dull and uninspiring. An uncut diamond looks very much like a pebble and most people would not give it a second glance. But, when cut and polished by the skilled hands of a craftsman, it comes alive with a brilliance and sparkle unequalled by any other stone. It is the cut of the diamond that enables it to make the best use of light, and the beauty of a diamond depends on the way it reflects light.

In the absence of light, diamonds are like the moon—cold and dark. But when the sun's rays strike them, they are transformed.

Just as a diamond is considered most beautiful when it is many-faceted and can bend light in virtually endless variety, the shape of our friendships also depends on the cutter—the friends who rub against us and play their lives against ours. Each diamond and each person reflects light a little differently.

A lonely person is a diamond in the dark. He knows nothing of his radiance and true character and serves neither God, others, or himself. But in the presence of special friends, the empty and lonely are changed forever. And the brighter the light of that relationship, the brighter the light the individual develops within himself.

One of the things that has made my life so rich is the wonderful relationships I have experienced. My family and friends have provided me with so much love and beauty I consider them my inner light or invisible diamonds. They are a part of the inner radiance which warms me and keeps me smiling. My relationships with others give me an inner sparkle and beauty that I hope shines much brighter than the diamond jewelry I find so much fun to wear.

But there is one friend who illuminates my life more than any other. Of all the friends I can claim, of all those whose light shines brightly, the brightest of all is Christ. His is a light which never falters, is never dim. He says, "I am the light of the world: he that followeth me shall not walk in darkness, but shall have the light of life."

The Son of God, more than anyone, sees our individuality and uniqueness. He does not demand anything of us but that we merely reflect His light wholeheartedly, that we be exposed to Him continually, that we be polished by Him constantly. "Let your light so shine before men, that they may see your good works, and glorify your Father which is in heaven," says Matthew. Our radiance, our brilliance, our glory, is a reflected glory warming and brightening us as we absorb it. And the source of that light will not go away. If exposed to it long enough, it becomes our own.

✦ *The Greatest Friend of All* ✦
· ·

*I*n this book I have shared with you the importance of the gift of friendship. Developing, maintaining, and cherishing friends is the key to a happy, fulfilled life. However, meaningful relationships are only temporal without a relationship with God. Occupations end, pleasures end, "raising" children ends, friends change, and sometimes end. All the diamonds and material possessions in the world cannot substitute for a lasting and fulfilling friendship with Him. My relationship with God is far more valuable than any of my resources. . . .

> Lord, you are more valuable than silver,
> Lord, you are more costly than gold,
> Lord, you are more beautiful than diamonds,
> And nothing I desire compares with you.

A wonderful gift has been offered to us, the gift of friendship with the greatest Friend of all, but we must accept it. A Friend who is more beautiful than diamonds, a Friend who created the diamonds and the world in which we live, a Friend who offers us the gift of eternal life.

✦ *The Conditions of a Good Gift* ✦

*F*or the real good of every gift, it is essential that the giver be in the gift—as God always is, for He is love—and, next, that the receiver know and receive the giver in the gift. Every gift of God is but a harbinger of His greatest and only sufficing gift—that of Himself. No gift unrecognized as coming from God is at its own best: therefore many things that God would gladly give us, things even that we need because we are, must wait until we ask for them, that we may know whence they come: when in all gifts we find Him, then in Him we shall find all things.

GEORGE MACDONALD

✦ *Friend of Friends* ✦

*H*e is the King of kings, the Lord of lords. And He is the Friend of friends. Out of His magnificent power and glory Jesus gently kissed away the tears of the heavy-hearted. He reached out in kindness to touch and tenderly heal the hurting.

He gave the gift of life to a weeping mother and taught His followers a better way to live. He let the loved disciple rest his weary head on His heart. He was their Friend, with all its richest meanings. He met their needs and allowed them to meet His. He was the Friend of friends. He loved. "Greater love hath no man than this, that He should lay down His life for His friends."

MARY HOLLINGSWORTH